TRUE CRIME
BAY RIDGE

———

Henry Stewart

ISBN: 978-1979234689

Slightly different versions of these stories were first published on the website Hey Ridge.

heyridge.com
henrystew.art

Cover design by Michael Verdirame for Silent Salesman.
Photo shows Thomas McFarland, right, with a detective, outside 360 Marine Avenue, in 1935. See Chapter 6.

For Sam

The Victims

The Victims
(continued)

TRUE

CRIME

BAY

RIDGE

1

Charley Ross

John Holmes Van Brunt was waked at 2 a.m. by a burglar alarm. It was a cold and wet morning in December 1874, and he lived on Shore Road, close to present-day Fort Hamilton High School, on the south side of what's now Shore Road Lane, on property his family had lived on since the seventeenth century. It commanded "a lovely marine view," Peter Ross writes in *A History of Long Island*, "one of the most sightly, beautiful and well appointed in its vicinity." His house stood across a narrow lawn from his brother's summer home.

Judge Charles Van Brunt had closed it up for winter, but not without first installing a telegraph that would alert his brother across the way if anyone tampered with the doors or windows. That night, "this alarm-bell rang violently," according to an account by Christian Ross. This wasn't unusual; sometimes a strong wind would blow a blind open, so John asked his son Albert to check it out.

Before Albert left, he stuck a pistol in his pocket.

He saw a light flicker in the window of the judge's house, so he returned home, told his father and got the family gardener, who lived nearby. The men also roused a hired man, Herman Frank, while John gathered his guns and joined them, even though he was seriously ill. Albert and the gardener stood in front of the house; John and Frank took the rear—and they stayed in position for almost an hour, watching the burglars' lights occasionally flash as they made their way through the judge's rooms. The only other light would have been the moon's; back then, there were mansions and homesteads along Shore Road, but the area was still largely farmland, Bay Ridge still a village.

John could only stand so much; it was damp, and cold, so he told Frank to open the back door. The housebreakers heard him fumbling with the key, extinguished their lights and started up the cellar stairs. The unfastened cellar doors, through which the burglars had broken in, flew open. Two men emerged, right into John and Frank; Van Brunt ordered them to halt, to which the thieves responded with gunshots; both missed. John answered with his shotgun and hit the man in front. "A cry of agony followed," Ross writes. The second trespasser fired again and ran—right into Albert, at whom he fired twice but missed. As the man kept running, John hit his arm with a shotgun blast, then got him again, in the back. He collapsed dead; his head fell atop his empty pistol.

The surviving housebreaker continued firing until his gun was empty, hitting no one. A neighbor, George Bergen, arrived with his brother and a hired man. The burglar asked for water—which Frank brought—and drank it. "You have got to die," Van Brunt told him. "If you have got anything to say, say it quick." Bergen asked the man his name. At first the man lied, gave some Irish name, but he soon admitted he was Joseph Douglas; his associate was William Mosher, of New York, a married father of five. Douglas asked to be buried with the $40 in his pocket, which he said he'd made honestly. And then he broke open the biggest mystery in the country.

"It's no use lying now," he said: "Mosher and I stole Charley Ross from Germantown."

Kidnapping for ransom is as old as history, but it was usually a side effect of battle. "Prisoners of war were frequently assigned a value and their fate determined by their family's or country's ability to pay a ransom," Richard P. Wright writes in *Kidnap for Ransom*. "The end result for those victims who were to be ransomed was the same as that of the kidnap victims today. They were forced to endure a period of captivity under often dire circumstances during which an amount to be paid for their freedom was negotiated." Ancient Jewish and Buddhist texts prescribe harsh punishments for kidnappers. So does Hammurabi's Code.

Still, kidnapping for ransom was unknown in the young United States. In the eighteenth and nineteenth centuries, there were a few cases of Native Americans abducting colonial children, but they were more often the spoils of battle, not means of raising capital. The case of American child abduction that endures in our collective memory is, of course, the Lindbergh baby (taken almost sixty years after Douglas made his dying confession), provoking a media frenzy and new laws by Congress. But it had a predecessor with similar details: a child, taken in the modern era, by strangers, who demanded a ransom for a child they never delivered.

The difference is—no one knows what happened to Charley Ross.

At 8 p.m. on July 1, 1874, an agitated Christian Ross left his home to find his two sons, who hadn't been seen for hours, and very quickly found one: Walter, who was in the company of a strange man. The Ross family lived in Germantown, Pennsylvania, a suburb of Philadelphia (now a neighborhood within the expanded city). Christian, an upper-middle-class dry-goods dealer, owned a two-floor stone house on the north side of East Washington Lane. "It stands on rising ground, about fifty feet from the road," he wrote in *The Father's Story of Charley Ross*; "the lawn is ornamented with evergreens and other trees."

That day, Christian's oldest children were with their grandmother, a hundred miles northwest in Middletown; his wife had taken their other daughter to Atlantic City. (After two weeks, Mrs. Ross was supposed to send the girl home and summon Charley and Walter; the boys were looking forward to it. "[I]n two of the letters from the abductors," Christian wrote, "Charley is represented as fretting lest he should not get home in time to join his mother at Atlantic City.") Many other people still occupied the grounds, including a cook, a gardener, two nannies and the Rosses' youngest—a baby girl.

That day, Charley, 4, had been playing with Walter, 6, on the road in front of the house. For the last several days, two men in a cart had passed and given the boys candy; on July 1, Charley asked them if they would give the boys a ride and buy them firecrackers, and the men agreed. Their father had said he would buy them some for the upcoming holiday, but Charley was 4 years old—he wanted them *now*. Walter sat on the passenger's knee, and Charley sat between the men; Walter asked to go to a nearby store, but the men said no, that they wanted to take them to "Aunt Susie's." The ride was long, and Charley cried. The men stopped at a cigar store at the corner of Palmer and Richmond in Philadelphia, six miles away, and sent Walter in with a quarter to buy firecrackers and torpedoes.

When he came out, carrying three small packages in his hands and four cents change in his pocket, he couldn't find the cart, or the men, or his brother. He looked up the street, down the street, around the corner. Then he did what most kids would—he cried, loudly, attracting a crowd, and a man brought him home. Walter thought *he* was the missing child, that his brother had been safely returned. But no one at the Ross home knew where Charley was.

His father reported the disappearance to local police, who told him it sounded like "a drunken frolic," and fig-ured the boy would be returned or found, abandoned, by patrolmen.

They were wrong.

The first note arrived on the Fourth of July. It was ad-dressed to Christian at his home, and it took some time to read—Christian not only had to decipher the sloppy handwriting but also the wanton, deliberate misspellings and dissolute grammar. ("you wil hav two pay us befor you git him from us, and pay us a big cent to.") The second letter, which arrived two days later, named a price: $20,000 [*very roughly, more than $400,000, adjusted for inflation*].

Searches began in multiple states, as far as a hundred miles away; canal boats were picked through, coal yards and outhouses searched, ferrymen and townsfolk questioned, from Trenton to Baltimore. Soon even the public was helping, combing over back roads, swamps and woodlands. Police searched Philadelphia building-by-building; they found nothing but false leads.

Local law enforcement officials told Christian he should not pay the ransom: "all united in expressing the belief that the threats would never be carried out, the object sought by the villains being money only," he wrote; "and that as soon as they should be satisfied that they could not accomplish this, the child would probably be left on the street or highway, and thence find his way home." Like the police who told him it was probably just a drunken frolic, these lawyers seemed unable to conceive of a child being ransomed, let alone murdered. Gossip in town suggested another, *real* motive; to many, the actual one was so absurd. (The public though was mostly sympathetic and moved by the Rosses' ordeal. There was even a popular song published, "Bring Back Our Darling.")

Christian and the kidnappers corresponded: he would reply with terse items in the personal columns of various newspapers, and the kidnappers would answer with threatening letters mailed to his home. They told him the price of $20,000 was fixed, and that the boy would die if it weren't paid. At least one well-to-do man offered to put up the money. But the family decided to follow the advice of the police and lawyers, though Christian struggled with his decision even as he remained resolute. "I would not compound the felony," he wrote; "hoping…that I will recover my child, and probably prevent a repetition of child-stealing for a ransom."

When the kidnappers discovered Ross wasn't as wealthy as they'd believed, they'd considered halving the ransom, but then still insisted upon the full amount because the public had been so touched by the story that they thought he could surely raise it. In another letter, they suggested that Ross could put Charley "on exhibition" when returned and make all the money back, because "there is not a mother in phila that will not pay a dollar to see him."

They weren't the only ones to have such an idea. Perhaps the most colorful scene in Christian Ross's book comes near the end, when he visits a carnival that has a wax model of "The Ross Family." Under a pseudonym, Ross is introduced to the owner, whom at length Ross then makes fun of—getting him to say things like, "Yes, I know Mr. and Mrs. Ross well….I have seen them often, and have been to their house"—before revealing his identity. The conversation ends with the carnival operator telling him, "When that boy's found I want you to let me have him to exhibit. He will draw better than anything I can get. I'll give you a thousand dollars a week for him for thirty weeks"—the ransom plus half.

The Rosses received twenty-four letters in all, the first half usually dropped in mailboxes or post offices around Philadelphia (though the kidnappers insisted the child wasn't in the city), the rest from New York, the Hudson Valley and as far as New Brunswick. In one, they wrote that, if the father would not pay, they would have to kill Charley so they could abduct another child and impress upon his or her parents how serious they were. The last letter arrived on November 6, more than four months after the kidnapping, postmarked Philadelphia. It reads like all the others, demanding the money be delivered in the next few days. Ross answered with two more personals, but he received no reply.

The authors would be dead in thirty-six days.

Detectives in New York broke the case as early as August, following leads about Mosher and Douglas, who had planned, according to an informant, to abduct a Vanderbilt child and ransom him in a manner very similar to what had happened to Charley Ross. Mosher and Douglas traveled the country selling a powdered moth poison called Mothee, and Mosher was also a boatbuilder known to frequent "the waters around New York in a boat on marauding expeditions," which is what brought the pair to Bay Ridge that wet December night (on a boat stolen in Bridgeport and modified by Mosher, possibly launched from 39th Street or Manhattan)—they were desperate for food and clothing, knew they were being hunted by police, that they were the most hated men in America, that they dared not show their faces in daylight or anywhere decent people congregated. Ironically, there was little in Van Brunt's house to steal. "They sold their lives cheaply," the Brooklyn *Eagle* reported in 1874.

Mosher was shot dead that night in Bay Ridge, and Douglas lay dying. He was questioned about where Charley was, and he told them only Mosher knew. They told him Mosher was dead, held up the body to show him, but Douglas swore repeatedly—he didn't know. He was in pain, and George Bergen, the Van Brunts' neighbor, gave him brandy and rubbed his hands. They tried to move him inside. "For God's sake," Douglas told them, "let me be." They wanted to put a blanket under him, but he wouldn't let them. He did promise that the child would be returned in a few days. "He remained conscious until about fifteen minutes before his death," Ross wrote. "Thus writhing in agony, lying on the spot where he had fallen, drenched with the descending rain, ended the purposeless and miserable life of one who aided in rending the heartstrings of a family unknown to him, and in outraging the feelings of the civilized world." It was about 5:30 a.m.

The bodies were brought to the morgue, and once the *Eagle* reported it, curiosity seekers arrived in large numbers to see the bodies. "It was the general remark of all who saw the face of Douglas…that he did not look like a bad man, in fact, he who would rather have been credited with the possession of some intellect," the *Eagle* reported. "No one seemed to pity Mosher at all. 'He's got a bad face' was the remark, and the reply generally came promptly, 'yes, he has, he's well out of the way'" (a nineteenth-century insult).

Walter was brought to the morgue in Brooklyn, on Raymond Street (now Ashland Place, in Fort Greene), and left alone with the bodies, no one telling or asking him anything, until he spontaneously recognized and identified Mosher's and Douglas's bodies as those of the men who had taken him and his little brother for a ride.

Everyone was convinced they'd caught the men who did it.

But Charley was still missing.

From the start, Christian was besieged by extorters and crazies. "Every person, both in the city and from other places, whose mind was not well balanced, or who was a monomaniac upon any particular subject, found us out, and proposed his way of discovering Charley." The most memorable was a man who explained, "God has punished you for cutting off your hair. He punished me, and two of my children died because I cut off my hair. You must not use razor or scissors, but let your hair grow, and all will be right. Your child will come back when your hair grows."

Letters arrived, insinuating possession of confidential information that could be purchased. Reputable citizens up and down the Eastern Seaboard sent word about every unattached child they saw, found or heard about— especially if his first name was Charley. Spiritualists offered advice from the other side. After the incident in Bay Ridge, Mosher's widow was uncooperative with police, but they were able to get from her that her husband said Charley had been placed with "an old man and woman, and was well cared for," but she didn't know who they were or where they lived. Suspicious elderly people were investigated and cleared.

According to a local rumor in Bay Ridge, Mosher and Douglas had lived in the woods of Brooklyn. Several farmers and Bay Ridge residents said they saw the kidnappers at a cabin on the hill that's now part of Sunset Park; one even said he'd seen a small boy there through an open door. But he'd asked no questions of the men, because they didn't seem "neighborly." This cabin was searched, but no evidence of Charley was discovered. "It was considered a peculiar coincidence, however," the Brooklyn *Eagle* reported in 1932, "that the cabin remained empty after the shooting of Douglas and Mosher." (Their boat was said to have been dragged ashore and kept for many years by "a local family" in Bay Ridge.)

Mosher's associates were rounded up, intimidated and released, because they knew nothing. Lost children were rounded up, interrogated and released, because they weren't Charley. Corpses were exhumed and reburied. Much of the public had concluded long ago that Ross was dead, but Douglas's promise that he'd be returned excited them anew. Even the family thought they might spend Christmas with Charley.

But Charley Ross never came home.

Though Ross's case was extraordinary for the ransom demanded, it revealed that abductions weren't so rare. Endless cases arose regarding suspicious men and women traveling through towns with children that weren't theirs. The most vivid of these was the story of Henry

Lachmueller, Jr., a 7-year-old boy found in Chester, Illinois, with two men, one of whom claimed to be his father. Local authorities, with the Charley Ross case fresh in their minds, didn't believe them, and eventually the boy told them his tale: that he had been abducted from a yard near his father's house, rowed across a river, hiked through the woods, beaten so he would stay awake, until they reached a cabin; then he was forced to beg, beaten if he failed to earn at least a dollar, which the men and a female companion drank up each evening. They wandered the Midwest like this until the woman died, and the men landed in Chester. The boy couldn't remember his name, his father or what town he'd come from, and his face was disfigured from acid, his back scarred, his hair crudely dyed. When his father read a newspaper account of the lost child, he traveled the sixty miles from Saint Louis. "What was his joy on seeing the child to find his hopes realized, and his long-lost son found at last," Christian Ross wrote. "The child had forgotten everything relating to his family, yet as soon as he saw his father he recognized him."

Christian Ross explored all such leads. He recounted several in his book: meeting with shady characters in saloons and hotels in New York, getting used in petty underworld vendettas; bushwhacking through the rural backwaters of north-central New Jersey to find families so isolated they'd never even heard of Charley Ross; bouncing around New York and Vermont bordertowns, looking for a clock-tinkerer who when he was drunk had called his son "Charley Ross," because the local boys were taunting him as such. All children with a slight resemblance to Charley Ross began to be called Charley Ross, and it became a catchall term for missing children. In his book, Christian tells a story about a boy and girl who wandered from their homes and were brought to a police station. An officer asked the boy, what's your name? "Charley Ross," he said. The officer asked the girl the same question. "Charley Ross," she said.

In February 1875, Pennsylvania made kidnapping for extortion a felony crime with serious penalties; before, no one had envisaged the need for such a law. The mayor of Philadelphia also declared a thirty-day immunity from charges relating to the Ross abduction, because the kidnapperes were dead. But no one came forward, except more people with lookalike children, impossible similarities and impossible stories, each dismissed after investigation.

Christian Ross kept eliminating possible Charleys until he died, in 1897, at which point his wife continued, until she died in 1912. In 1926, two years after the fiftieth anniversary, the house was torn down and replaced by the Presbyterian church that's still there. Walter kept up the search after his parents died; he and his sisters still received letters from middle-aged men, claiming to be their long-lost brother.

The most famous was Gustav Blair, who came forward in 1934 to say he was Charley Ross. The 64-year-old carpenter said he was "kept in a cave when [he was] a small child and afterward adopted by a man who told him he was" Charley Ross, the Pittsburgh *Post-Gazette* reported in 1941. Two years before, a court had declared that Blair *was* the missing Charley. "This man's claims are entirely unfounded and we intend to ignore the action of the court," Walter told the Associated Press. "Blair is evidently just another one of the cranks who have been bothering us for the last 65 years. The idea that my brother is still alive is not only absurd, but the man's story seems unconvincing." The Rosses had given up hope by then, sixty-five years after the abduction, that Charley would ever be found alive.

So no one knows what happened. Maybe, like the Lindbergh baby, Ross was killed the day he was taken, but buried somewhere and never found. Maybe he was kept hostage on a crude boat, or in a remote cave, and when his abductors were killed, he died of thirst. Maybe his face was deformed by acid, and he was raised by strangers in filth. Maybe he forgot his name, forgot which city he'd lived in, forgot his father and his mother and his sisters and Walter. Maybe he lived and died on an isolated back road, or was spirited between dustbowls until he was old enough to drink himself to death. Or maybe he was there the whole time: maybe he was an Arizona carpenter who had been saved from a cave, or another one of the boys that Christian saw and dismissed maybe too quickly, not taking seriously enough how abduction and confinement could have changed a boy.

In the Shirley Jackson story "Louisa, Please Come Home," a runaway returns years later but is rejected by her family, who are convinced she's an impostor, especially because she's the third girl to show up at their house, claiming to be Louisa. "My daughter was younger than you are," her father tells her. At some point, skepticism curdles into cynicism.

Except perhaps among the credulous general public. The Internet is full of people whose grandfather was Charley Ross—everyone in the family knew *that*.

In March 2013, a Philadelphia librarian was going through family artifacts when she discovered a stack of old letters, which she assumed to be love letters. Then her daughter read one.

"Mom," she said, "these are ransom letters."

The family had no idea how or why it had acquired the Mosher–Ross letters, *Smithsonian Magazine* reported. But, on the advice of the rare manuscripts man at a Philadelphia auction house, the family put them up for sale at the end of that year. The final bid was $16,000; with fees, the cost came out to $20,000—the same price Mosher and Douglas had once charged for Charley Ross himself.

2

Frederick Hardy, John Kelly & Mary Kelly

Captain Aumack spotted the body, floating in the water. It was about 8 a.m. on Thursday, November 2, 1899, and he was out on his oyster sloop in Raritan Bay, a mile and a half off the coast of Keyport, New Jersey—and about twelve miles southwest of Fort Hamilton. Aumack "ordered the boat to be brought alongside" the floater, the New-York *Daily Tribune* reported.

> The crew drew the body into the boat with boathooks, and when it reached the deck they were amazed at seeing a rope tied about the waist, attached to which was a stone weighing...thirty pounds. The skull was also found to be crushed in and the face badly bruised.

Around the neck was a purple mark, indicating the man had been strangled or the body had been towed through the water after being thrown overboard.

His pockets had been turned out, and he had no money, watch or wallet. But the coroner, examining the body, found written on his undershirt, in indelible ink, "Frederick Hardy, jr., Mount Pleasant, Tennessee."

Though it wouldn't have been immediately apparent—a Southern body, found in New Jersey—this murder mystery would be traced to the dark, forested roads of Bay Ridge; before it was solved, decades would pass.

And the killer would strike twice more.

Keyport officials had been notified to look out for Hardy, who had disappeared almost two weeks before. (He's not to be confused with another Frederick Hardy, young locksmith of Bay Ridge, who in 1874 had shot himself on the street, through the heart, because his wife had cheated on him.) Hardy had been boarding on the southern end of what we now call Bay Ridge but what was then still the village of Fort Hamilton, a bustling vacation destination that had grown up around the armybase—with a reputation by that time for rowdiness and heavy drinking. One magazine reporter, in 1894, had called it "a shabby section…afflicted with evil resorts and abounding in brawling throngs."

An autopsy concluded that Hardy had been murdered, by a blow to the head. The likely motive was robbery, as he may have had as much as $40 on him [*very roughly, $1,125, adjusted for inflation*], as well as a unique cigarette case, made of gun metal, almost the color of a rifle barrel, and an unusual watch, all of which were missing.

The watch had belonged to Hardy's grandfather, Henry C. Hardy, a banker who lived at 111 Montague Street. "It was made in England," the Asbury Park *Daily Press* reported, "and was of guinea gold. It was a combination watch of peculiar make, as manipulation of a spring would remove the outer cover, and from a case watch the piece would be transformed into an open face one. The case was worn thin, and Mr. [Henry] Hardy doubted if there was another watch in this part of the country like it." The newspapers believed that if it were discovered—say, brought to a pawnbroker or jeweler—it could crack open the case.

But it never was.

What did turn up were cards and receipts belonging to Hardy. Annie George lived at her late father Henry's house, on Shore Road and 99th Street, which about thirty years later would be demolished and replaced by an apartment building. (Henry, an influential economist, had died suddenly, in 1897, at the peak of a momentum-gathering mayoral campaign; his friend and neighbor Tom L. Johnson's house later became Fontbonne Academy.)

A 1931 photo shows a dignified, three-story colonial home with a handsome colonnaded porch. Across the street, Annie (and a search party of friends) discovered "seven cards, five engraved with the name of young Hardy, lying scattered about the ground on a steep declivity leading from the Shore Road down to the water's edge...opposite the home of Albert Johnson [Tom's brother], the street car magnate, at Ninety-ninth Street and the Shore Road," the New York *Times* reported.

> When a reporter called at [George's] house hoping to find some one who had heard cries along the lonesome road [Annie] guided him to the spot where the cards had been noticed. On the water side of the Shore Road opposite Mr. Johnson's house there is an opening in the railing left

for a gate, but to which no gate is swung. From this opening steps lead down the declivity twenty feet, whence a zigzag pathway leads southerly to Mr. Johnson's boat-house. From the foot of the stairs the path sheers almost straight down to the water's edge. The hillside is covered with trees and bushes, and is a desolate place. At the gateway at the top of the declivity lying just inside the rail from the street a card with young Hardy's name on it was found. Lying just within the rail on the other side of the gateway and within a few feet of the street was found the bloody card bearing the young man's name. It was crumpled.

Six finger marks were outlined on the face, across which was a spatter of blood. Down ten of the wooden steps was picked up a Pullman sleeping car receipt for passage from Tennessee to New York.

Hardy had moved north to attend the Art Students' League, a still-functioning school near Carnegie Hall; he was scheduled to begin classes on Monday, October 23—the day before he disappeared. (A man at the school told me it doesn't appear to have records that go back that far.) Hardy had chosen the Fort Hamilton area because T. Coleman Ward, his inseparable "chum" from college, in Nashville, was living there with his aunt, Mrs. E. C. Moxham, on 96th Street, between Shore Road and Marine Avenue. Hardy had found a room in a boarding house nearby, on Shore Road and 95th Street.

He spent his last day living it up, Fort Hamilton style. "The young men engaged themselves in various ways, bowling, cycling, boating, and fishing, and Hardy became known by sight to many of the residents of Fort Hamilton," the *Times* reported. Another report suggests he did a bit of bawdying. In the afternoon, he bought three packs of cigarettes at McNickles Pharmacy, on Fourth Avenue. Later, he visited the Bismarck Hotel, the Martin House and the Dewey Hotel. "He stayed a short time in each place and, it is said, was seen to drink several glasses of beer," the New York *Journal and Advertiser* reported. There was a rumor he may have been with a woman, but the Dewey Hotel registry contained no handwriting that resembled Hardy's.

The boys were back at the Moxham house that evening, with some other young people; Hardy remained until about 11:15 p.m. "His manner was much as usual, and he talked of his ambition in art, sang, and played, and seemed in the happiest of moods." When he left, a young man "gave [Hardy] his card, and invited him to call," the *Times* reported. "Hardy took the card and put it in his vest pocket. He was accompanied to the door by his friend Ward and bidden good night.

"He was never seen again...by any of his friends."

"Not many minutes later Hardy must have been felled by his murderer," the Asbury Park *Daily Press* surmised, "who, after rifling his pockets, carried the body to the water, tied the stone about the waist and probably towed

the body out into the bay near where it was found."
(When accumulated gases finally pushed the body to the
water's surface, the corpse was "very much decom-
posed," the Brooklyn *Eagle* reported, "and had evidently
been in the water for some time.")

"It was a moonlight night" when Hardy disappeared,
the Virginian-*Pilot* reported. "Between the Moxham
house and Hardy's boarding house there were four street
lamps burning. Hardy never reached the boarding
house."

He probably hadn't gone that way. He'd told his
friends that, because he'd been smoking so many of
those cigarettes he'd bought earlier at McNickles, his
mouth was dry, and he thought he might walk down to
the village proper—south of 99th Street—where he
could buy some gum. He may have also wanted more
cigarettes. His friends came to believe that Hardy had
gone "across the vacant lot at the corner of Ninety-sixth
street and Marine avenue; thence down Third avenue
and Ninety-ninth street to the store where he was in the
habit of buying both chewing gum and cigarettes," the
Eagle reported. ("This store...is in the rear of the Fort
Hamilton post office," which at the time was on the corner of 99th and Fourth, putting the shop approximately
at today's 9820 Fourth Avenue.)

The only problem was, "The man who owns and
tends the store tells the *Eagle* reporter that Hardy did not
come there on the night that he disappeared. Of this the
shopkeeper is positive. He says that he knew Hardy from
having often seen him with Ward, and he says that he
kept his store open that night until around midnight.

"Hardy left the house on Ninety-sixth street at about 11:10 o'clock, and at an ordinary pace, he would have reached the store within ten minutes, probably less."

If he had gone to another store, or the shopkeeper was mixed up, many believed Hardy would have walked to Shore Road and headed north, and that, between 99th and 97th streets, he would have met his murderer. The killer would have stood in front of him, right-handed, and struck him on the head—likely with a blackjack, and not a club or a rock, because the skull wasn't fractured. This blow would have killed him instantly, rupturing blood vessels in the brain, producing the one-inch-square blood clot Hardy'd suffered. "The practice commonly followed by thugs who commit such crimes is to spring upon their victims from a shadow or approach suddenly from different directions," the *Eagle* reported. "One man seizes the victim and holds him, or, at least, engages his attention while the other delivers the knock-out blow."

Then these killers would have emptied his pockets and carried him down to the Hegeman boathouse, just south of the Johnson boathouse reached by the stairs at Shore Road near 99th Street, where the cards and receipts had been discovered. Hegeman had twenty-one boats for rent that season and no nightwatchman; several used stone anchors like the one tied to Hardy, and one was missing. The killers must have rowed him out to sea from here, then dumped him and rowed back, storing the stolen boat so it didn't arouse suspicion.

Then they would have fled.

*

Frederick Hardy, Sr., promptly came north from Tennessee when he heard his son was missing. "He has been scouring New York and vicinity, but could not even find a clue," the Asbury Park *Daily Press* reported—that is, until he read an item in a New York paper about the "ghastly find" in New Jersey. He took the early train to Keyport with his father, Frederick's grandfather. "At Undertaker Beele's place he asked to see the body," the Chicago *Tribune* reported.

> "It is my son," said the father, shaking with grief and horror at the marks of the terrible end of his son. The father, as he stood by the mangled body and saw with what a ferocious cruelty life had been crushed out, announced a determination to have vengeance.

That evening, Hardy's body was sent to Norfolk, to be buried in the family plot there. It arrived in the morning via the New York, Philadelphia and Norfolk Railroad, accompanied by his father and grandparents. (His mother and sister had helped Hardy install himself at the house on 95th Street before sailing to Europe, which is where they were when he disappeared and when his body was found.) The funeral was held at the grave, in Elmwood Cemetery, where it remains today, marked by a plainly engraved stone.

"His father said that the young man had no enemies, and was of the sort who made friends rather than enemies," the *Daily Press* reported. "Apparently the police are all at sea, and the father said that there could not be found a person in the neighborhood who heard even a cry for help on the night of the murder."

Because the handrail of the stairs that led down to the boathouses was broken, many surmised that this was where Hardy had struggled for his life; and because it was where the cards had been discovered, many believed it was the scene of the murder.

But the Brooklyn *Eagle* wasn't convinced. First of all, because Hardy had no injuries besides the blow to the head, he may not have put up much of a struggle; there was a good chance he was killed before he knew what hit him. Furthermore, "to have committed the murder on the Shore Road at this point, near Ninety-seventh street, would have been a desperate and dangerous act," the paper argued. "To have searched the clothing and thrown away the articles as the body lay on the edge of the much traveled Shore Road would have been ten times more so."

Instead, the *Eagle* suggested that the killers would have examined more closely what had been taken from Hardy after they'd disposed of his body, returning to the road from the waterfront, tearing up and tossing out his cards as they went. (Police were also, in other ways, skeptical of the cards, believing they "had not been there any length of time, as they showed no weather stains," the *Times* reported. They might have even been kept by the killers and scattered about as "a blind," except more evidence had been found at the boathouse, including

Hardy's wallet and possibly his hat, strongly suggesting that the killers had shoved off from and/or returned to there.)

The *Eagle* believed instead that the killing had been done elsewhere. The best theory was Marine Avenue, between 96th and 97th streets, the path he would have traveled to get to the store at which he'd never arrived. This road "is heavily shaded and the foliage at the time of the disappearance was thick enough to have made the path pitch dark," the paper reported. "It would have been a desperate undertaking to carry the body of the young man to the water front from this point, but after all no more desperate than to have assaulted him on the Shore Road and to have searched his body where it fell."

Shore Road at this time would have looked and felt quite different from the way it does now. Landfill had not yet extended the coast; there was no park as we know it today. Still, it was "one of the finest and coolest shades in the vicinity of New York," according to an 1887 guidebook. "It is bordered by handsome villas set amid artistically laid out pleasure grounds. Here the overhanging majestic trees interlace their broad foliage, and the observant spectator will note a thousand beauties in this charming thorough-fare where art and nature both unite to form a picture of perennial beauty."

Though surely in the dark of an autumn night, such verdant charm could have seemed malevolent. "At this season of the year the [area] is nearly deserted," the Virginian-*Pilot* reported. "There has been some complaint recently by people of the vicinity that rough-looking men have been loitering along the Shore road..., having taken refuge here from the activity of the police in the borough of Manhattan."

Tramps were common to old Shore Road. "Come when you will along the Fort Hamilton road, and you will always see a tramp or two either reclining under the shade of a wide spreading beech tree surveying the glad waters of the Narrows, or else with his back against a tall cedar, taking huge bites out of a colossal sandwich," the *Eagle* reported in 1886. As late as 1934, when Victoria Muspratt was murdered in her crumbling mansion on the other end of Shore Road (see Chapter 5), police considered that the culprit might have been a tramp, especially because one had been spotted in the area, "whose shabby garb and shifty eyes made him conspicuous," the *Eagle* reported.

Many, including Frederick's father, believed one or more tramps to be responsible for Hardy's death. "A resident of Fort Hamilton...said that he had seen a party of tramps acting suspiciously on Fort Hamilton pier on the morning of Oct. 23," the *Times* reported. "The tramps seemed to have money, as they made frequent trips to a near-by saloon."

> One of the tramps was a tall, slender man who wore a reddish-brown checked suit. He left the others, and, going to a point on the shore where it is believed the crime [could have been] committed, spent some time in searching apparently for something. The informant thought that the man may have been trying to make sure that no clue had been left that would aid

in the detection of the murderer or mur-
derers.

Such anonymous, possibly scapegoated tramps weren't
the only suspects. A sailor was arrested on November 5
and released the next day for a lack of evidence; he admitted to being on a launch with a friend that landed
that night at Hegeman's boathouse but said they were
only there to enjoy a few hours' carousing. He "was in-
dignant at his arrest," the *Times* reported.

Another man, a former gunner at the armybase
who'd lived in the village for years, knew the area, the
boathouse and where needed supplies—such as ropes
and anchors—would have been kept. "He may be innocent," the *Journal and Advertiser* reported, "but there is a
strong chain of circumstantial evidence against him."
There's no indication he was ever arrested. Then there
was the vague reporting in the *Eagle* and *Times* about an
old, unsolved crime in another state that strongly resembled the Hardy case, and that police had determined the
same man was behind both and were now pursuing him.
They don't seem ever to have caught him.

Other odd stories and possible connections followed,
as they often do in mysterious murder cases. A woman
wrote to the *Eagle* to say her brother, Robert Francis
Clark, who lived at 88th Street and Gatling Place, had
disappeared in September. "She fears her brother met
the fate that befell young Hardy," the paper reported.
"There is a suspicion that there is an organized band of
highway-men which frequents Fort Hamilton." A report

the next day suggested Clark wasn't actually missing, and I could find no more mention of him.

The Hardy case, once so closely followed that even no news made the news, disappeared from the papers for the next two years—until Martin Bennett died. The wealthy local resident had seen "strange men" at the dock that Hardy's killers would have left from on the night he died. Bennett told friends he had more information that could lead to the killers' capture, the *Eagle* reported.

> It appears that the death of Mr. Bennett was caused by apoplexy, brought on by an animated discussion between a strange man and himself. The stranger appeared on the Bennett premises and he and Mr. Bennett had been heard to use harsh words. The stranger disappeared a few moments later, but not before he had informed the next door neighbors that Mr. Bennett had been taken suddenly ill and needed assistance. It is expected that should the stranger be located he might be able to throw some light on the Hardy mystery.

But, like every other lead, nothing came from this one, either. The case remained cold.

Until two more people were killed.

In 1906, John Kelly worked as a driver at the Crescent Athletic Club, Brooklyn's most prestigious sporting and social institution, whose summer grounds were where Judge Charles Van Brunt once lived (see Chapter 1)—where Fort Hamilton High School is today. He was 45, and he lived with his 24-year-old wife, Mary, and their two young children, Annie and Mabel, in two furnished rooms in a two-story frame boarding house on Dahlgren Place, near 92nd Street.

It was supposed to be temporary; Kelly had recently been evicted from his home in "Irishtown," a nickname for a part of Fort Hamilton Village, and moved to his friend's boarding house in the woodsy Goose Hill section, the area "behind" the armybase, from about Fort Hamilton Parkway to Seventh Avenue, as far north as 86th Street.

John Kilbride was 25. He "worked a little and idled a great deal," the *Times* reported, and he "hung about the [boarding] house much of the time. Kelly did not like this."

Their antagonism reached its climax on Tuesday, June 5, 1906. The boarders often got together in the evening, as they had this night. "Drinking was indulged in freely," the *Eagle* reported, "and before morning the party became rather boisterous and disorderly." John Kilbride and Mary Kelly were present, but her husband was not—he had another engagement. That left the two paramours alone to talk (and possibly to do other things?), which they did for much of the night.

Then John Kelly came home, preceded by the sound of his footsteps. "Here comes your husband!" someone shouted. Mary begged her lover to hide. The *Eagle* reported that he refused, but the more colorful account in the *Times* says he obliged.

> Kelly apparently had some knowledge that Kilbride had been about. He immediately began upbraiding his wife for encouraging him. Mrs. Kelly resented being publicly scolded, and a quarrel ensued. Suddenly Mrs. Kelly, the police say, cried out:
>
> "Well, it's true, I love him!"
>
> It is not very clear what Kelly started to do. Before he could say or do anything Kilbride had jumped from his hiding place and was between Kelly and his wife.
>
> Kilbride said...that Kelly had jumped at his throat. By the looks of his face and throat, he did. Kilbride, however, had a revolver in his hand. He fired three shots, according to the police. One of them hit Kelly in the heart, another, a stray shot, hit Mrs. Kelly in the chest, and still another went wild.
>
> A soldier from Fort Hamilton was the first to reach the house after the shooting. He notified the police, and told them when he got into the place those in the house were going right on drinking their beer, although the body of Kelly lay on the floor, and Mrs. Kelly, mortally wounded, was lying on a bed in her room.

Annie, 5, and Mabel, 2, were sent to the Children's Society.

Kilbride had run out the back door, and he was not arrested until morning. (Reports vary as to whether he gave himself up after spending the night in Coney Island or was captured near the village by detectives.) Mrs. Kelly was taken by ambulance to the nearest medical center, Norwegian Hospital, on 43rd and Fourth, but succumbed to her injury on June 10.

The following day Kilbride faced a second charge of homicide. And the day after that, a grand jury indicted him for murder in the first degree; realizing he could get the electric chair, Kilbride agreed that same day to plead guilty to murder in the second degree, and he was sentenced to twenty-to-life at Sing Sing.

He could be a troublesome prisoner. In September 1913, Kilbride was seen working in the prison's shipping department at 3:45 p.m. But fifteen minutes later, when the guard began to gather the men to return to their cells, Kilbride could not be found. From where he'd been, "there was little to prevent a prisoner from slipping out of the building," the *Times* reported, "except the fact that when he did get outside there would be nowhere for him to go." Guards said no gates had been opened for him to slip through, no fences unwatched for him to climb over. "The authorities are not certain whether he has escaped or is hidden within the walls."

"He is five feet seven inches high, and weighs 180 pounds," the *Times* added. "He has blue eyes and brown hair. On the left side and back of his head are several scars and two teeth are missing on the left side." His prison clothing was marked with the number 56,471. He no longer much resembled the man the *Eagle* had once described as "well dressed and attractive looking."

It turns out he'd made it only twenty-five feet. The warden ordered an intensive search of the shops, believing Kilbride couldn't have escaped the prison grounds. (Just a month earlier, an inmate had hidden in the clothing shop for almost a week.) The guard in the packinghouse poked every shaft several times; eventually, a tin cup rolled out of one. "Soon after that his probe encountered something soft, and then there were wails from a man inside," the *Times* reported. "Kilbride must have lost his hold as the result of the jabbing, for he shot out of the shaft to the floor like a weight.

"He was taken to a cell."

This boneheaded escapade took place about six weeks after Kilbride had sent a letter to a Sheepshead Bay policeman, confessing to the murder of Frederick Hardy, Jr., almost fourteen years earlier. "The signature to the letter is 'John Gilbride [sic],'" the *Eagle* reported, "and the writer states that he is the John Gilbride who is serving a life sentence for the murder of John Kelly and his wife at Fort Hamilton in June, 1906."

> According to the police, 'Gilbride' says that his conscience bothers him and he wants to 'clear off the books' the mystery of the murder of Hardy. The writer goes on to state that he was down financially and seeing Hardy display a roll of bills he followed him, struck him with an ax and

> after robbing him threw the body in the
> bay, weighting *[sic]* it down with a stone.

Gilbride/Kilbride would have been about 18 when Hardy was murdered. There's no indication that police had considered him as a suspect—unless he was a tramp and owned a reddish-brown checked suit.

And there's not much more mention of this letter in the press, at least that I could find: whether police took it seriously enough to officially close the Hardy case, or even whether it was confirmed to have been written by Kilbride. (Unlike the *Times*, a few other papers at least mentioned the confession in their accounts of Kilbride's Sing Sing nonescape.) Maybe he really killed Hardy; the letter strikes me as too specific and random to have been a hoax. But an imaginative mind could conjure reasons for him to have lied: perhaps some renewed pressure on the police to close the case was displaced onto Kilbride, who agreed to cop to the murder in exchange for some reward, such as better treatment in jail? He was in for life, anyway—or so he would have thought.

No one appears to have taken this letter seriously enough to file it with corrections officials. Ten years later, on June 24, 1923, John Kilbride walked out of Sing Sing, inexplicably paroled after serving just seventeen years for a double homicide, three short of his minimum sentence, even though he had *tried to escape* and *confessed to a third murder*.

The *Eagle* reported, in a tiny item near the bottom of page 20A, that he was "in joyous mood" as he left—and then he disappeared into history, along with his victims.

3

Daniel Maloney

Sgt. Johnny McGarty worked at a police station on Hamilton Avenue, since torn down for the BQE, but he lived in Bay Ridge. He had just gotten off the thirteen-year-old Fourth Avenue subway at Bay Ridge Avenue, dressed in plainclothes, on March 19, 1929, at approximately 1 a.m., when he heard the gunshots, first two, then six more—"a regular volley," he later said.

> I ran down [69th Street, toward Third Avenue] and I saw a man chasing another man and firing at him. There were others dodging here and there, and there was lots of shooting.
>
> I shouted that I was a policeman, but maybe they didn't hear me. Anyway, the two men dodged into a storm door and I went in after them. [McGarty saw the man with the pistol bending over the other man, who had been wounded in the leg...McGarty ordered the man with the pistol to throw up his hands. "Instead...he swung around and fired point blank at me. He missed, and I emptied my pistol into his body."] I fired four times and he toppled over. The other man jumped by me, and he fell just outside the door.

I had to rap the revolver out of the hands of the man who had fallen. He looked up at me and mumbled, "I'm a cop."

Naturally I bent down over him, and he said, "I know you, you're a sergeant in the 39th." Then I asked him to tell me what had happened, and he asked me to get him a priest. He wouldn't tell me a thing. He stuck out his hand, though, and I shook it.

The dead cop was Patrolman Daniel Maloney, of 576 77th Street, and he "was certainly not doing police duty," the police commissioner said the next day. Maloney had been at a meeting of supposedly rival bootleggers at the Owl's Head Tavern, a café and speakeasy on the northeast corner of 69th and Third, now a coffee shop. (In March 1929, prohibition had been the law for nine years, its repeal was still four years away, and the stock market wouldn't crash for seven more months.)

Charles "Vannie" Higgins had had his trouble with Tommy Connell, is what the papers said. Higgins was an above-average gangster, a Bay Ridge native known as the "czar of Brooklyn liquor interests," though he strongly denied it. "The fact of the matter is," the Brooklyn *Eagle* later explained, "that Higgins rose from the status of a mere taxi operator, that he now owns a fleet of cabs, that he has a great interest in aviation, and that he operates two seaplanes, both of which seem able to fly only at night." (Higgins lived in an apartment at 7420 Ridge Boulevard, to the consternation of his neighbors, who feared the violence he attracted would one day follow him home.)

Connell, Higgins's supposed rival, was a "quiet, sedate young man [with] an interest in bootleg liquor in the same section." Higgins and Connell had met, investigators believed—at least at first—to hash out their disagreements. Higgins brought a few friends, and they all brought their wives, the *Eagle* reported, "to make Connell certain that everything was all right."

But it wasn't. The bartender at the Owl's Head said Patrolman Maloney showed up and demanded to speak to Connell; a shot was fired indoors, and then Maloney pulled Connell out into the street. "After that on the street the shooting became general." More than sixty shots were fired by the time the gunfight was over. Everyone ran. Connell "couldn't have escaped," the *Eagle* reported—he had been shot in the right leg, probably by Maloney. "He tried to crash out of a storm door which hides the side entrance to the Tavern, and crumpled up at McGarty's feet," the *Eagle* reported.

One of Higgins's associates was arrested at the scene, and Higgins himself was captured on 69th Street. He'd been hiding behind a parked taxi, which almost ran him over when it pulled out with "a highly excited policeman" in the backseat "who wanted to make sure he caught somebody in all that fracas." (This incident was later cited in a letter-to-the-editor as a reason not to legalize overnight street parking for automobiles—because it offered a hiding place to gangsters!) "Higgins insisted he was running away for protection. [A responding officer] pointed out that if he was afraid of the shots he'd have ducked for a doorway. So they took him to the Fort Hamilton station," the *Eagle* reported. Other associates escaped.

Another man, from Bensonhurst, was also shot; he "felt the sting of a bullet in his left leg as he was walking to a rear room of the tavern from the bar," he later testified. But police believed he was an innocent by-stander. "The shot, [the victim] said, was fired from outside."

This short-lived blaze of barking bullets became known (briefly) as the Battle of Bay Ridge, a bona fide, beer-fueled gang war and tabloid sensation. Connell, Higgins and his associate were arrested and arraigned the next day. "This trio, appearing diffident and looking misjudged...all pleaded not guilty...and all were held without bail," the *Eagle* reported. "Then Connell, who had been limping around all day, came near to swooning because of his wounded leg. They sent him to Swedish Hospital."

Bail was later set at $5,000 [*more than $70,000, adjusted for inflation*]. Higgins and his man posted it, left together in a car and disappeared.

Maloney, the dead patrolman, seemed to be the key to whatever had happened. He was found with four revolvers—one in his hand, two in his pockets and another in his holster. "He had no right to be where he was shot," the police commissioner said. "We cannot understand why he had four revolvers on his person...He certainly had no police reason for carrying so many guns." Another firearm was "as wicked-looking a sawed-off shotgun as one would want to see" with "a heavy curved handle and two short, ugly barrels." It was found near Connell. "He had no ammunition for it, however," the *Eagle* reported. "Maloney did. A box of cartridges for the gun were in his pocket. The gun most certainly had been discharged, too, because when [an officer] picked it up it was still smoking."

One of the pistols was a police service revolver that didn't belong to Maloney—its serial number was 9969, or maybe 6966, so the men associated with both were brought in for questioning. But the weapon belonged to a different cop, who'd resigned three years earlier and convinced investigators that his gun had been stolen a year after that.

Detectives believed Maloney had been with Connell at a different speakeasy, on 69th and Fourth Avenue, before the shooting, where they'd been drinking— though friends later said Maloney never touched liquor. Connell left with Higgins's peace party but without Maloney. "It is certain that Maloney went to the Tavern carrying a young arsenal, but whether *he* started the shooting or not is something that hasn't been determined," the *Eagle* reported.

> However, it is true that in the general firing no one was hurt. It was only when McGarty came that the deadly shooting seems to have begun. Up to that time a great many guns had been fired, but when the police began their roundup the only ones they could find were the revolvers Maloney had...all 38-caliber, and the sawed-off shotgun.

In fact, no one could (or would) say they saw anyone shooting but Maloney. The felonious assault charges against Higgins, Connell and the other man were discharged after the trial, in April 1929, at which the nine witnesses who testified, including four cops, said they hadn't seen anyone else do any shooting. Still, a week and a half later, cops raided the Owl's Head Tavern and found ten half-barrels of beer in the cellar; the waiter was arrested, and a co-owner was followed to and arrested at his home in Midwood, where "a large quantity of assorted liquors" was confiscated.

Regardless of all this negative attention, the Owl's Head Tavern remained open at least into the 1960s.

An odd aside: a few months after the trial, in August 1929, in Long Beach, Long Island, a man was shot at the Indoor Yacht Club, at Ocean Front Street and Wyoming Avenue. Police afterward were looking for "Handsome" Thomas J. Slattery, also known as "Big Tom," "well-known and feared some years ago along the Brooklyn waterfront," the *Eagle* reported, as a honcho in the Ironworkers Union. He was also once co-owner of the Owl's Head Tavern, and the rumor was that the victim was a stool pigeon for Prohibition Agents, though authorities denied it.

The victim gave his name as Edward Thomas but his real name was Thomas E. Russell; he staggered into the local station house after midnight and requested medical attention. The bullet had entered his body above the heart and "glanced off the spine." Russell told the cops that Slattery had shot him, and that several other men had been at the club when he was shot; police blew a siren blast, the signal to raise Long Beach's drawbridges (its main traffic exits), and they remained up until guards could be posted.

Slattery's car was in front of the club, but he wasn't there; no one was. Slattery wasn't at home either. He was caught the next day, but Russell dropped the charges a week later from Long Beach Hospital, when it became clear that he'd live. (He was subsequently charged with perjury.) Slattery was immediately re-arrested for running a speakeasy, and he died two months later of hemorrhages, in connection with an operation a year earlier to remove a rib.

In the 1940s, the Vannie Higgins story was featured in the first issue of *Crime and Punishment*, a true-crime comic book dedicated to the "eradication of crime." It even featured scenes from the Owl's Head shootout, hilariously rewritten so that Maloney is an honest cop who just happens to be on the scene; McGarty accidentally shoots him when a bullet meant to scare Higgins ricochets off a plate. "Poor Maloney," the ghost of a different cop, who's trailing Higgins, says over the patrolman's dead body. "He's got a couple of kids, too!"

No one believed that's what had happened, but the truth remained uncertain. The dominant theory was that there had been "a break in friendship" between Maloney and Connell. "It may be…that Maloney was afraid of what might happen if Connell patched up his troubles with Higgins." Then again, "There are men about town who say that Tommy Connell and Vannie

Higgins...never would have held a peace conference such as seemed to be going on when the guns began to bark," the *Eagle* reported.

Higgins had been known to the police before the shoot-out, having been arrested eight times. He was convicted twice, of assault, in 1915 and 1916, both times placed on probation. Otherwise, his cases were discharged: in 1926, for assault, then for robbery; in 1928, for possessing a revolver, for homicide, for grand larceny, for felonious assault and again for homicide.

Higgins died three years later, shot by Murder, Inc., agents on Union Street, just west of Prospect Park, as he was walking with his family, including his 7-year-old daughter, after her tap-dance recital, around 1:30 a.m. It made the front page of the *Times*, which called him a "rum runner, night-club owner and most powerful underworld leader in Brooklyn since the death of Frankie Uale." He's buried in Middle Village, Queens.

As soon as Higgins was let off for the Maloney incident, "he went to Baltimore," the *Eagle* reported. He "has been making that city his headquarters ever since. He has returned to Brooklyn every now and then, but for some reason...he comes in very infrequently, and when he does arrive it is without a brass band or advance notices."

> It has never been fully explained why Tommy Connell...who was not friendly with Higgins, should have been in Owl's Head Tavern with

> the latter that night. Connell was doing pretty well in a business way, and was cutting in a little on the business of Higgins. Why a peace conference should have been arranged, if it was arranged, under the circumstances, is a mystery that has baffled the detectives. They are also wondering why every one went to [a] peace conference carrying a gun.

"Police are investigating...but they are getting no help from those who know what it was about....Since none of [those arrested] will talk, and since their wives profess to know nothing, and since two other men who were in the party couldn't or wouldn't tell much, the rest is entirely supposition..."

"There are lots of things they don't know, and lots of things they probably will never find out."

One thing we do know is that Higgins gave his address to police as the Hotel Stafford, which the *Eagle* reported was in Manhattan, on 93rd and Third. The paper was mistaken: surely it meant the Hotel Spafford, actually at that corner in Brooklyn—the old name for the Prince Hotel.

4

John Arthur Russell

John Arthur Russell was 8 years old in September 1932, one of 1,500 students at St. Anselm's—likely a third-grader, though the newspapers never specified. The school, at 83rd Street and Fourth Avenue, was then just five years old, and at that time it let its students out for lunch, at noon. Russell was walking alone the half mile to his home, at 114 81st Street, as he usually did; he was about halfway, on the corner of 81st Street and Third Avenue, when two men stopped him.

"Are you the little Russell boy?" one asked. They both had mustaches.

Yes.

"Well, your father's sick and he wants us to take you to his office," one said, gesturing to a car parked nearby.

"Unsuspecting," the Brooklyn *Eagle* reported, "the lad entered the car"—even though the Lindbergh baby had been abducted just six months earlier.

While one man drove, the other blindfolded the boy, then wrapped him in brown paper up to his eyes. They drove for almost an hour and a half, stopping once at a stationery store to buy two picture books—and to place a ransom call. Afterward, when the car stopped again, "one of the kidnappers tucked the youngster, like a large package, under one arm and carried him" into an apartment house, the *Eagle* reported.

The men told Russell it was the Hotel Pennsylvania, across from the old Penn Station. But really, it was less than two miles from his house.

The Russells' home phone rang at 12:40 p.m. The maid had been sent out to look for the boy, so Mrs. Russell answered.

"Your child is kidnapped," a man's voice told her. "Have $25,000 ready in small bills." [*Almost $438,000, adjusted for inflation.*]

She became hysterical, and the caller said he'd call back—but he wouldn't for more than seven hours. Mrs. Russell called her husband, a partner in a Manhattan stock-exchange firm, McClure, Jones & Co., who called the police before coming home. (The firm was where employees Margaret Fogarty and Henry Rudkin had met back in 1919; they would marry and move to a Connecticut property they called "Pepperidge Farm," after which Margaret would later name her bakery.)

The next call came at 8:15 p.m., and the kidnapper spoke to the father, Arthur S. Russell, who kept the kidnapper on the line while police tried to trace it. The kidnapper sounded desperate—he lowered the ransom to $10,000, then to $2,000; then he became suspicious that the call was being traced and hung up.

But police had already traced it, to one of five phone booths in a candystore at 8604 Fourth Avenue. By the time they got there, though, the caller was gone, and "the proprietor was not able to recall who had been using his booth," the *Eagle* reported.

*

That night, before midnight, three women saw a boy, "frightened, chilled in the night air," the *Eagle* reported, again on the corner of 81st and Third. They were telephone operators who worked nearby, likely at the phone-company building on 77th and Third, and had just clocked out, at 11:30 p.m. Aware of the kidnapping from the late editions, they asked him if he were missing.

"Yes," he said. "Take me home."

John Arthur Russell was reunited with his parents about eleven hours after he'd been abducted.

He was unhurt, but his kidnappers were still loose.

The next day, the police chief inspector took the boy around Bay Ridge, hoping they could find the place where he'd been held. The boy said he'd been in an apartment. For several hours, a "nice man" had read to him, picture books with Wild West and Mickey Mouse stories. They gave him chocolate bars, sandwiches and milk.

From a window, young Russell could see a vacant lot, where children were playing in a brown tent. This lot, and this tent, were the police's best clues.

A woman, married to a cab driver, called her local police station, because her husband's taxi license needed to be renewed. While talking with the desk lieutenant about it, the Russell case came up. He told her about the tent.

"It's a funny thing," she said, "but I live in an apartment house, and from my window I can see the same kind of a tent the little boy described. Wouldn't it be awful if it turned out that the kidnappers had lived in the same house?"

Of course, they had. The apartment building was and still is the most out-of-the-way in all of Bay Ridge— 293 Dahlgren Place, at the corner of Fort Hill Place, then-nestled on a secluded, dead-end street, surrounded by the Fort Hamilton armybase (part of which is now the Verrazano Bridge off-ramp) and Poly Prep.

Elmer Grafton had rented rooms there, the landlady said, but he had been in it only a few times since then, with another man.

Lately, no one had seen him.

Grafton was a phony name. The apartment had been rented by George T. Clarke, 26, of 449 51st Street—the "nice man" little Jackie Russell had mentioned. Clarke's accomplice was Allen W. August, 35, of 1116 Ditmas Avenue; he'd made the phone calls.

Clarke was from Cleveland and returned there after the boy had been released. Police suspected his involvement, though didn't explain why to the papers, and tapped his phone. On Tuesday, October 11, 1932, he told his wife he would return the next day.

Police were waiting for him at the train station, where he was arrested. August was arrested at the same time, at his home in Brooklyn.

The two weren't exactly Mosher and Douglas, the men who'd kidnapped Charley Ross. Both were young Brooklyn businessmen, each with a son just older than John, but they had fallen on hard times—as had many

Americans in the years following Black Tuesday, 1929. "I was desperately in need of cash," August told police, "and Clarke was broke and without a job. I owed the insurance companies a lot of money which had to be paid by the 20th, and I simply did not have it to pay. Clarke and I talked things over and decided the only way to get some ready cash quickly was to kidnap the child of some well-to-do family."

They drove around Brooklyn on September 8 and saw Russell, playing; they inquired about his family and found out the father was a wealthy Wall Street broker. They learned his schedule and waited.

The public, which had been rabid, was suddenly sympathetic. Even Mr. and Mrs. Russell had lost their bloodlust. "When Jackie was taken…I felt I could shoot these men on sight—if I ever saw them," he said. "But now it is different. It is a sad case. I wouldn't want to see them sent away for years if I could help it. I don't believe they knew what they were doing. But now, of course, the case is not in my hands. I am only a witness."

"It is too sad," Mrs. Russell said. "You cannot hate these men. They have no police records. They have never done a thing like this before. They are both fathers. There is no satisfaction in prosecuting them. It is too sad. But the case is out of our hands."

"They bought me candy and cookies," the boy said, "and they drew pictures for me all afternoon. Finally when I cried for mother they let me go home." The men had been spooked by the massive police response, and afterward drove the boy to 77th Street and Fort Hamilton Parkway, with directions on how to get home.

Russell didn't quite follow them; he wound up at 72nd and Fifth, where he was discovered by a woman who'd gone out to the drugstore, around 11 p.m. He told her he'd been visiting his uncle—he didn't want to tell his story to strangers, he said later—and she put him on the Fifth Avenue trolley, and told the motorman to let him off at 81st Street. Russell walked from there, meeting the telephone operators who brought him the rest of the way.

A reporter found Clarke's aunt "standing in the toy-filled vestibule of his basement apartment," the *Eagle* reported. "We've lived here 43 years with never a blemish on our name," she said. "We can't understand what would have got into George.

"Money, of course. It went to his head."

Both men reportedly confessed to police, yet pleaded not guilty—Clarke's lawyer, in fact, pleaded "not guilty on the ground of insanity." As anecdotal evidence, the *Eagle* reported, "Clarke's mother...had mortgaged her home so as to put her son into the insurance business with Allen W. August....Shortly after that business connection was made...Clarke worked out plans for what he called a worldwide insurance company, with which most of the world's greatest figures were to be connected, and of which he was to be head.

"Nothing ever came of it."

By December, August had also pleaded not guilty by reason of insanity; his lawyer said that at the time of the crime August had suffered "a mania-depressive illness."

The judge agreed to appoint a commission, but he didn't believe the claims. "In my opinion these men are sane and were sane on Sept. 19 when they committed the kidnapping," the judge said. "Rest assured they are going to get prison sentences. They are going to Sing Sing. But you are entitled to your full day in Court, so I will appoint a commission of alienists," or psychiatrists.

In the end, the two agreed to plead guilty to attempted kidnapping, which had a less severe sentence than kidnapping, and the district attorney accepted. A week later, the judge sentenced both men to four-to-twenty-five years in Sing Sing. "Should both men behave," the *Eagle* reported, "it seemed likely yesterday that they would be paroled after serving three and a half years."

The once clement Mrs. Russell had again hardened. "No sentence could have compensated the anguish I suffered while Jackie was missing," she told the *Eagle.*

"I have absolutely no sympathy for these men," she later added. "I am afraid no child will be safe when potential kidnappers see how lightly such a crime is regarded." As she spoke, John Arthur Russell, who'd been playing in the background, wandered forward, and the reporter asked him what he thought of the kidnappers' punishments.

"He wrinkled his small brow as if trying to recall how the two strange men had looked," the *Eagle* reported.

"'Oh, I guess what Momma says is right,' he said finally. 'I don't care, anyway.

"'I remember they bought me some candy.'"

5

Victoria Muspratt

In 1928, Eugenia Muspratt, named after the last empress of France, was found dead of a heart attack in the cellar of her Shore Road home. After that, her sister Victoria never again ventured downstairs. "Upstairs," the Brooklyn *Eagle* reported a few years later, Victoria "lives in what might be called squalor. The ten-room house is festooned with cobwebs. There is no plumbing, no water, no heat and only the light of a lantern."

"I am not a pauper," Victoria told the paper, "but I cannot bear to miss the glorious sunsets, the moonlight which traces a path of silver on the water in front of my windows and, most of all, the home that was my father's."

John Muspratt was born in Liverpool, made a fortune in New Orleans and settled in Bay Ridge in the mid 1840s—to invest in real estate, and make even more money. He owned a yacht, named for Victoria, which he moored at the foot of 71st Street. After he died, in 1880, he left his daughters the house at 7059 Shore Road— well, two houses, actually. There was a smaller one in back of the one that fronted Shore Road, where Victoria had been born. The family lot extended almost all the way to Narrows Avenue.

The back house was described, like the main house, as "a weatherstained frame house tall and boxlike in a severe architectural style," and "architecturally like a matchbox on end, [making] an eerie figure in the night." Muspratt rented it out for $5 [*almost $90, adjusted for inflation*] to a spinster named Miss Hannigan, or possibly Rattigan. The front house, by the 1930s, had a "leaky mansard roof [rising] behind a row of scraggly lilac bushes, about twenty-five feet back from...Shore Road"; it resembled a classic haunted house, the kind kids dare each other to approach. And its inhabitant, Victoria, was a classic eccentric: she was 4-foot-10; she had rheumatism in one leg, and high blood pressure, but she still hobbled up to Our Lady of Angels for mass every morning she could.

The Muspratts had owned land onto which Poly Prep was built in 1917 but had sold it—or maybe they'd lost it by not paying taxes, or maybe Victoria's heirs had actually inherited it; the stories differed. Whatever the case, it was the Shore Road property Victoria prized. She liked to watch the boats in the Narrows and could name every one. She said she could tell what the next day's weather would be like by the way the sun set over Staten Island. Goats once pastured on her lawn. "At the northwest corner of the house, rising squarely above the roof, is a tower," the *Eagle* reported. "It is designed much after the fashion of London Tower. Inside is a winding stairway. At the top is one bedroom."

She dressed oddly, in old clothes, and used old furniture but owned no bed; she slept in an armchair by a window. She was a hoarder, among whose possessions in 1934 was a season pass for Coney Island from 1890. She harassed local beat cops; she once asked one for pencil and paper, looked at his shield, noted its number, and said, "I'm going to report you. You laughed at me." The policeman found the piece of paper among her things after she'd died.

She also used a crutch ever since she'd been discovered one Saturday evening with a fractured leg and lacerations to her scalp in front of 7211 Shore Road, unable to recall how she got them when detectives interviewed her in her Kings County Hospital bed. That mysterious accident was a brief sensation in late 1920s Bay Ridge—police later considered it a simple automobile accident—titillating newspaper readers with headlines such as "Mystery shrouds hermit found injured in roadway." Many at the time knew little of her, or even that she lived in the house—even that she was still alive!

She once notoriously rejected a $175,000 offer for her house [*approximately $2.75 million, adjusted for inflation*], which helped fuel speculation that she had money hidden away. So did the story of Richard Muhlmeyer, a bus driver who'd once helped Victoria put out a fire (several of which damaged the house in its final years); he stopped by several times thereafter to check in on her, and at Christmastime, 1931, she stopped him as he passed and pressed an envelope into his hand. It contained $25 [*almost $400, adjusted for inflation*]. The *Eagle* reported:

> The bus driver was so surprised that he went to a druggist friend and asked if it was real. When he told the druggist who had given it to him, the former said:

> "She could have given you $100,000
> [*$1.5 million, adjusted for inflation*] and never
> missed it."

But she didn't have a secret fortune; she was just a generous old woman who'd rejected the offers for her house so she could die where she'd always lived. Construction on some of Shore Road's first apartment buildings had begun in 1931 across the street, Nos. 7101 and 7119. "Although Shore Road property is being bought up with amazing rapidity for apartment house sites, the little old lady holds fast to her own," the *Eagle* reported. "And will, she says, with fervor, to her dying day."

That day arrived—but not from natural causes. "Miss Muspratt...lived in fear of...an attack," the *Eagle* reported, "because of neighborhood rumors that she hoarded a fortune in her squalid surroundings." A neighbor said Victoria was "especially worried because her voice had become so feeble and she would not be able to be heard if she tried to shout for help."

Just before Christmas in 1934, a few months after the paper reported the house was being fixed up a little, the 72-year-old Victoria was found dead in her "tumbledown, refuse-littered shack," her crutches beside her, her body on the floor near the chair where she slept; her throat had been slashed, according to initial reports, or maybe not; police later surmised that two axes found in the cellar, where her sister Eugenia had died, had been used to crush her skull, underneath which were found thirteen old gold coins.

Investigators were greeted at the house with "the musty odor of clothing of the hoop-skirt vintage, newspapers and magazines more than a century old," the *Eagle* reported, "and antique furnishings piled helter skelter among dust and cobwebs....Rats scurried about. Maps of the old towns of Fort Hamilton and New Utrecht were turned up."

"Every room of the house of death was crammed with curios," the AP reported; "seventy-five-year-old magazines, yellow newspapers, creaky furniture, a wheezy organ or two; even a letter once carried by pony express." A one-hundred-piece set of china, made in London in the 1830s, was found "ornate and complete ...covered with dust on an upper floor, to which Miss Muspratt's crippled condition had denied her access since 1928.

"Like the house, the surrounding grassless plot was covered with debris."

The day after Christmas, hundreds of people could be found loitering during the day near the old mansion, "looking curiously at the dilapidated house with its bare windows and weatherbeaten walls. Passing autos slowed down to a crawling speed as the occupants filled their eyes with the scene of mysterious death of the aged woman."

Most believed the motive had been robbery; a set of keys Victoria wore around her neck, for various closets and strongboxes, was missing. But one neighbor said Muspratt would often come to dine at her house because she didn't have enough to eat; she would borrow change to drop in the collection at church, because she didn't have any. (Two bankbooks found in the house did show some savings, including $2,343 [*almost $42,000, adjusted for inflation*] at Brooklyn Savings Bank.)

Police had a few suspects. Because of the coins found under her head, a man who worked at a newsstand at 77th and Third, who had tried to sell an old gold coin to an acquaintance following the murder, was twice taken in for questioning—and twice released. A man who had chopped firewood for fuel for Muspratt several times was sought for questioning.

Police also entertained the idea that a tramp had beaten her to death "after a squabble which might have followed her refusal to give him as large a handout as he demanded," the *Eagle* reported. A tramp had been spotted in "the exclusive Shore Road residential area last week." He was described as "a prowler whose shabby garb and shifty eyes made him conspicuous."

The police tried to connect a man who admitted to robbing houses in Bay Ridge and Flatbush to the murder, but it didn't stick; the crime remained unsolved.

Muspratt's house turned out not to be worth much. The estate sold at auction in 1936 for just $18,150 [*approximately $325,000, adjusted for inflation*], despite the much higher offer she'd once received. Muspratt, it's said, had wanted to donate the land to Our Lady of Angels, though this was apparently not in her will. The Catholic Church, however, did eventually take the land—today, it forms a part of the plot on which Xaverian High School sits, just around the corner from Barkaloo Cemetery.

6

Florence McVey and Nora Kelly

Patrick Murray heard the dog barking, which wasn't right. He worked as a train conductor for Brooklyn Manhattan Transit and had come home from his shift close to 4 a.m. on April 1, 1935; he lived on the second floor of a house at 360 Marine Avenue, above an elderly woman, Nora Kelly, who about 10 p.m. each night usually unleashed her "soft-eyed crossbred collie" and let him into the cellar. But there was Brownie in the backyard, "straining at the rope that bound him to the fence," the *Eagle* reported, filling "the raw night air with lamentations," as the *Times* put it.

"When the feeble rays from Murray's flashlight were trained on the kennel, the rope was already frayed and Brownie was leaping against the noose in frenzied efforts to get loose," the *Times* continued. "He was quivering as Murray untied him."

> The dog virtually dragged the conductor around to the front door, scratching the gravel walk in frantic attempts to make better speed. His paws rasped on the little stoop as he led Murray into the dark hallway, toward the cellar stairs...
>
> Brownie's body palpitated as he threw himself against the cellar door.

He scratched at it...At the foot of the stairs Murray recoiled in horror. The golden glow of his little flashlight etched the black-clad figure of [his landlady, Kelly, a] gray-haired woman hanging limply from one of the rafters ten feet away, with her white face staring toward the ceiling. Behind her, where the weak light failed, deeper darkness.

Brownie whimpered and leaped at the figure, apparently mystified by the unresponsiveness of his mistress. His bushy tail drooped, he went flat on his stomach as he lay there, whining....Murray wheeled, the cellar went completely dark as he hurried upstairs, but the dog kept its vigil in the blackness.

Murray called the police from a nearby coffee shop on Fourth Avenue, and they arrived within minutes. Cops cut down Kelly's body, as Murray held back the frantic dog, then moved on to the apartment upstairs. "On the [kitchen] table they saw a platter of meatballs and onions, part of a loaf of raisin bread, a half-finished glass of milk and two coffee cups, one full, one empty except for dregs," the *Times* reported. Kelly's worn, black-leather purse was also on the table, with just her house keys and rosaries—no money. The kitchen faced the backyard; like the cellar, it was hardly in disarray, nor was the adjoining dining room. "As [detectives] stepped across the threshold of the [front] parlor, they traveled across old papered walls with a few old pictures, a few simple but much worn chairs and tables and then traveled across a worn flowered carpet," the *Times* continued.

> In front of a green cretonne-covered sofa that is backed against the dining room wall, facing out toward the porch, lay [Kelly's granddaughter] Florence McVey. She was on her back and her head was tilted to one side. Sightless eyes were fixed on the ceiling. She, like her grandmother, was fully dressed except for her shoes.

Wearing a brown skirt, silk stockings and a gray V-neck sweater, she looked like she'd died in her sleep; there were no visible bruises. An early theory was that maybe Kelly, 68, had hanged herself, and McVey, 18, found the body and had a heart attack, staggering upstairs to die.

Kelly didn't have many visitors to her home, which no longer stands near the corner of Fourth Avenue, and recently it had been unusually empty. Years ago, one of Kelly's daughters had died while giving birth to twins, and ever since Kelly had been raising those girls, now 11, and their older sister, 14. But a few months earlier, their father, Thomas McFarland, had fought with Kelly, taken his daughters and moved out.

The old lady was, though, often visited by her granddaughter McVey, on Thursdays and every other Sunday. She was described in the newspapers as "a vivacious girl" with "beautiful chestnut hair," a graduate of nearby St. Patrick's parochial school who had done two years at the all-girls Bay Ridge High School (at Fourth Avenue and 67th Street, now Telecommunications) before dropping out to start working. She had landed a job as a domestic for a family with two daughters in a house near Fort Hamilton Parkway and 90th Street. She "was quiet, shy and reserved," her boss told the *Times*. "She stayed in nights, had no beaux and was devoted to her grandmother. Whenever she got time off she would spend it at home with her grandmother."

Kelly had raised McVey, too. The girl's father disappeared when she was nine-months-old, and her mother, another of Kelly's daughters, gave her up. "I didn't have any money," the mother told the *Eagle*, "so I thought Florence would be better off with my own mother."

An autopsy revealed McVey had been smothered, either by pillow or by hand. Investigators then rushed the old woman's body, which had been sitting at the local precinct, to the morgue, and an autopsy found that her lungs had collapsed, possibly from a powerful blow, maybe around 6 p.m., and then she was strung up, possibly to confuse investigators.

Both had been raped, though no newspaper quite said so.

The house was a crime scene. Police began questioning relatives and neighbors, including everyone in the huge apartment building across the street, but no one—not even Murray's wife and child and dog, who were sleeping upstairs until roused by the commotion the train conductor had created—had heard anything.

"While police and reporters came and went, Brownie, the collie, was still howling in the cellar," the *Eagle* reported. "He was put in his doghouse and kept there until the A.S.P.C.A. wagon arrived.

"He fought violently against the attempt to take him away but was overpowered by sheer strength."

It didn't take long for detectives to find the killer. Kelly had a friend, Eleanor Myers, who lived about half a mile away, at 142 Gatling Place. She'd walked over to Kelly's home Sunday evening at 9 p.m. According to the *Eagle*:

> She knocked on the door, and, receiving no answer, turned the knob and put her weight against the door. She could only open the door a few inches, she said, because a chair was backed up against it. As she turned to leave, she [later] testified, [a man] came to the door and stepped into the hallway.
>
> "Is Mrs. Kelly home?" she testified she asked...
>
> "I guess she's at church," she said his answer was. They stood in the hallway chatting for a few moments.
>
> "Is Florrie home?" she said she asked.
>
> "No. I'm waiting for her myself to come home..."

Myers had seen this man at Kelly's home several times before—he was Thomas McFarland, 38, Kelly's son-in-law, father of the three girls Kelly had raised for almost a dozen years before the recent quarrel. (What that had been about, no one was quite sure.)

McFarland was arrested at 5 p.m. Monday, less than twenty-four hours after the murders, as he left his job in Long Island City at Paragon Paint and Varnish. He was fingerprinted, then interrogated for four hours at the Fort Hamilton police station. (When a patrolman delivered McFarland's fingerprints to police headquarters in Manhattan, he encountered on the steps a man with a gun, which the gunman pressed to his own temple, "determined to die to gratify his curiosity about life beyond the grave." The patrolman disarmed him.)

McFarland denied he'd even been at Kelly's house, but there was blood on his clothing. (He "wore a soft gray hat, gray suit, blue overcoat and soiled blue shirt with blue and white necktie," the *Times* reported.) He finally, calmly, confessed, around 10 p.m. There was "absolutely no reason at all, no motive" for the killing, he told his questioner. "I didn't know what I was doing."

Mostly because, he said, he was very drunk.

McFarland had dinner with his three daughters around 3 p.m. that Sunday. He had met their mother in 1917, when he moved from his hometown, Mobile, Alabama, to begin duty as a private at Fort Hancock, New Jersey, on Sandy Hook, during World War I. They were married that year at St. Patrick's church, on 95th and Fourth, where McVey had gone to school, just blocks from Kelly's home.

Seven years later, Mrs. McFarland died. Thomas and his girls now lived in Williamsburg, at 236 Humboldt Street, probably a slum, because the building was torn down within a year for a public-housing project— the Ten Eyck Houses, now the Williamsburg Houses. During dinner, McFarland drank a beer, and a glass of sherry, he later said. Then he left for Kelly's; he stopped at a saloon, where he drank five more glasses of beer.

Then he got on the subway and presumably exited at the 95th Street station, opened a decade earlier, and walked the rest of the way, arriving at the Marine Avenue home at dusk—close to the time of the murders, according to investigators, though McFarland said he'd killed them hours later, around 8 p.m.

He'd brought a bottle of sherry with him, and he drank several glasses of it at Kelly's home. The old woman finally told him to "stop drinking," he said later, "and making a hog of myself." Kelly and McFarland were in the kitchen—McVey was lying on a couch in the parlor, two rooms away—when the fight escalated. Kelly lifted a chair, to strike him, and he killed her. He wasn't quite sure of the details. "Everything went black before me," he said. But he must have struck her, hard, in the chest; he likely strangled her as well. Then his niece came into the kitchen. "See what you've done!" she said.

"There was a knife on the kitchen table," McFarland said. "I was afraid the girl was making for that knife. I knew that she knew what I had done, so I grabbed her and choked her until she was unconscious. I carried her back to the living room. She was senseless then."

He left her there, returned to the kitchen, picked up Kelly and carried her down to the cellar. He'd noticed the telephone wire in the cellar in the past, when going down there to clear away ashes. But he didn't remember, he said, stringing Kelly up, so he could never explain why he'd done it.

"I didn't have anything in mind," he told his interrogators about his visit to the house that evening. "I was just going for a visit. I certainly meant no harm to Florence, only I suddenly realized I had to get her out of the way because she was a witness."

"I got my hat and coat," he finished, "left the house about 9 o'clock and was home again by 10 o'clock."

As he told his story in the Fort Hamilton Station, his daughters—Marian, 14, and Anna and Edith, 11—sat nearby, in another room. "He told the story [of the murder] with no show of emotion," the *Eagle* reported, "and his outward calm was only broken when he learned that his three daughters were waiting."

The *Times* described his reaction: "a wince of something akin to pain flashed across his sharp features and he shook his dark mop of hair in a hopeless gesture." The girls were brought to the Children's Society Shelter, on Schermerhorn Street, awaiting a decision by children's court. The three were now officially "neglected children."

McFarland, meanwhile, "was taken to the scene of the crime after his confession to re-enact it," the *Eagle* reported (a photograph from which appears on the cover of this book). That took less than an hour.

"Then he was locked up."

*

There are large gaps in McFarland's story, as it was printed in the press. The word "rape" rarely appeared in the Brooklyn *Eagle* in the mid 1930s, and almost never in a hard-news story. This was true of newspapers in general; the industry's preferred euphemisms were "criminal attack" or "criminal assault." "Consequently, we were obliged to write such fatuous sentences as 'He kicked her down the stairs and beat her with a stick but he did not criminally attack her,'" journalist Jack Smith once explained in the Los Angeles *Times*.

Prosecutors planned to charge McFarland with what was called "felony murder," meaning that the killings happened during the perpetration of another crime—the rape. "Both women were criminally attacked before they were killed," the *Eagle* explained (or rather, didn't). It had reported almost the same thing in the second paragraph of the very first story about the case: "Both [women] had been criminally assaulted before being attacked." So did the New York *Times*: "Both women were criminally attacked before their death, according to findings of physicians."

Front Page Detective, a true-crime magazine later adapted into a television show, ran an article about the case in its December 1936 issue, clarifying the matter by calling McFarland "Brooklyn's Lust Killer."

From the general outline of the newspapers' account, you could almost recognize something sympathetic in McFarland. Many men don't like their mothers-in-law; the two had been fighting lately, young children were involved. Obviously he meant no harm to the niece, who was just in the wrong place at the wrong time. Right?

Except, when McFarland said, "I carried her back to the living room. She was senseless then," the elided conclusion of that sentence must be, "and then I raped her as she died," suffocating her when he was finished. Perhaps she had interrupted him as he was raping his former mother-in-law, Kelly's grandmother, to whom he then returned for some reason, to drag her raped and murdered corpse from kitchen to basement.

Kelly's and McVey's bodies were taken to 471 40th Street, the home of Helen Stiers, Kelly's daughter and McVey's mother. The murder had been on Sunday evening; the burial was Friday morning, April 5, at St. John's Cemetery, in Middle Village, Queens, following a requiem mass at St. John's, where years before McFarland had been married to Kelly's daughter. (Kelly and McVey were to be buried in the same grave; according to the cemetery's website, there's a Florence Mc Vey buried there, as well as three Nora Kellys, but none of the internment dates are April 5, 1935, and they're all in different sections of the cemetery.)

A funeral procession left Stiers's home, led by a police car; eight officers were on hand to keep order among the 200 people who'd assembled.

The motorcade reached St. Patrick's. "As the two caskets were being carried into the church," the *Eagle* reported, "a collie, resembling Mrs. Kelly's dog that first brought police to the Kelly home after the murder, twice tried to run into the edifice."

70

But Brownie wasn't permitted at mass.

McFarland was a sensation at his arraignment; elevator girls deserted their cars to get a look at him. He appeared before a judge "with his eyes averted and two red spots burning high on the cheeks of his pale, bristle-covered face," the *Times* reported. A clerk asked him how he pleaded to the charge of killing Kelly. He "hung his head and rolled his eyes upward in a fixed stare," the *Times* continued. "The prisoner's throat muscles flexed and his lips seemed to form the word 'guilty,' but he made no audible sound…Judge Taylor broke the silence. 'Not guilty,' he said, and McFarland repeated the words in a low tone."

These were capital offenses, to which he couldn't have pleaded guilty even if he'd wanted to.

McFarland's lawyers hoped to save him from the electric chair through a temporary-insanity defense. One of his attorneys, the president of the Kings County Criminal Bar Association, called McFarland a "raving maniac," following a meeting at the Raymond Street Jail, where he was being held. (It was once the borough's main prison, "Brooklyn's Bastille," closed in 1963; Raymond Street was later renamed Ashland Place.) "He refused to talk to me," the lawyer said, "except to continually complain of feeling dizzy. He refused to sit down because he said it made him dizzy and he repeatedly asked to be let out." McFarland was soon removed from the jail to Kings County Hospital.

When McFarland went on trial in January 1936, it was with a three-day beard. He "sat at the counsel table, staring vacantly down at the table top," the *Eagle* reported. "During all of the session he rarely changed his posture. His hands folded in his lap, his eyes glazed, McFarland, wearing the same gray suit he was arrested in, didn't even look up when [the assistant DA] called him a conscienceless killer."

He remained this way throughout the trial. A week into it, the *Eagle* reported McFarland "never has once shifted his position at the counsel table. Rocklike and immobile, he sits, head bowed, never moving, his hands clasped in his lap. He shaves only every three days."

His lawyer said that first day he "had no intention of denying either the crime or its heinousness," the *Eagle* continued. "He even stressed its revolting character in an effort to show, as he said, that no sane man could have committed it…[the lawyer said] McFarland was insane at the time of the slaying, was before, and still is."

A consulting psychiatrist agreed. This defense doctor said McFarland suffered from "equivalent epilepsy, a condition in which the normal processes of rational thinking [are] arrested, as the physical faculties are during ordinary physical epilepsy," the *Eagle* reported. His lawyers said he was shell-shocked from serving in what we now call World War I; "he was the sole survivor of the crew of a tank shattered by a German shell," the *Eagle* reported. Psychiatrists for the prosecution, however, testified that he was sane.

It would be up to the jury to decide whom to believe. It retired on February 5, 1936—without its foreman, who'd asked to be excused to help tend to his two sick brothers—and within two hours returned a guilty verdict, convicting McFarland of the first-degree murder of Florence McVey. (Kelly's murder wasn't prosecuted.) The mandatory sentence was death in the electric chair, though McFarland wouldn't be formally sentenced for a few more days. The *Eagle* reported:

> As he heard the verdict yesterday the 38-year-old widower, father of three children, did not emerge from the apparent stupefaction which has characterized his behavior all through the trial…As if in a dream, the World War veteran, whom a war buddy on the witness stand [described] as [a] hero, heard the verdict rendered. Silent and dazed, he then was led forward by two attendants to the bar to answer routine questions.
>
> To the stock questions of when he was born and where, did he drink any intoxicating liquors, are his parents alive, the defendant's only reply was:
>
> "I don't know."

McFarland was formally sentenced to die for McVey's murder on February 11, 1936, five days after the verdict was issued. He "heard the death sentence with the same dazed expression which he wore when the jury's verdict was returned," the *Eagle* reported. As he'd been led to the courtroom, he saw his eldest daughter, Marian, now 15, sitting in an office. The last time he'd seen her had probably been when she testified for him in his trial. *Front Page Detective* described that scene:

> [Young Marian McFarland] testified that he often was dizzy and "excited over nothing," that on many occasions he had got out of bed and gone out in the middle of the night. "When I would tell him about it the next day, he would say that he did not remember," she said.
>
> The defendant kept his head bowed and stared at the floor all the time his daughter was on the stand. When she was excused, she stepped down and walked to his side.
>
> "Daddy, please, daddy—look at me!" But he did not look up, and the girl was led out.

Now he asked to have a word with her. His guards cautioned him not to mention the almost certain death sentence he was about to face. But he did. "They can't do that!" Marian screamed. "They can't do that!"

McFarland tried to arrange to have his World War bonus paid to his daughter. Before he was sentenced, he had obtained the application; he did his best to fill it out, and handed it over to the Society for the Prevention of Cruelty to Children, who had taken charge of the children; the society's superintendent said he'd complete it.

McFarland left for Sing Sing from Grand Central Station with five other prisoners and three deputy sheriffs. "Before leaving Brooklyn," the *Eagle* reported, "he was taken to police headquarters to be photographed. His necktie was taken from him. The only personal possession McFarland took to the death house with him was a group photograph of his three children."

The execution was set for March 16, but appeals were filed, forestalling it until the Appeals Court upheld the conviction on July 8. McFarland died in the electric chair about six weeks later, on August 20, 1936, at the age of 39, following a steak lunch around noon and a final supper of roast chicken. Then, the prison chaplain "accompanied him from his cell down the corridor to the execution chamber. McFarland's lips moved in prayer, but his words were not audible," the *Eagle* reported. He "uttered no word when he was led into the death chamber at 11:03 p.m. He was pronounced dead four minutes later."

On his last day, McFarland told a reporter he was "all right and fit for anything." He had received no personal visitors. The warden had said McFarland could see his daughters one last time, but he "was reluctant to bring them to the death-house," the *Eagle* reported. He had last seen them three months ago, when they'd visited him at Sing Sing.

"I'm not worrying so much about myself," he told a reporter hours before he died.

"It's my three young girls I'm upset about."

7

Dorothy Carlucci

Dorothy and Eugene Carlucci, married for twenty years, left their home at 356 89th Street, one of a row of six-family houses, on Sunday, June 13, 1937. It was about 7 p.m., and they were going to see a movie with Dorothy's sister. They strolled the 1,500 feet to the Harbor Theater, on Fourth near 92nd (today a gym), where Dorothy realized, looking at the posters, that she'd already seen the feature picture there. So they walked down to Third Avenue and caught the trolley northward, toward the Bay Ridge Theater.

In the earliest days of cinema, sites such as beer gardens hosted roving exhibitions. The Bay Ridge Theater, opened in 1915, was the neighborhood's first proper movie theater, and it remained the grandest, with almost 2,000 seats. It operated in some way until the 1960s. The building still stands, on the northwest corner of 72nd and Third, repurposed as a gym, McDonald's and pharmacy. The theater is the setting of a raucous 1959 short story, "Double Feature," by Hubert Selby, Jr., who grew up across the street.

That night in 1937, there was also a double feature: *The Good Old Soak*, a now-forgotten B-movie with Wallace Beery, and *Personal Property*, a romantic comedy with Robert Taylor and Jean Harlow—who had just died the week before, prematurely, of kidney disease.

The threesome left the theater at about 10 p.m. Frank Lofrisco, a local patrolman, was on duty that night, guarding the theater's cashier, who was preparing to visit the bank with the day's deposits. Lofrisco was idling near the ticket window as he watched the three head down the street. Then he saw one of the women fall to the ground. She cried, "I'm shot! I'm shot!" He rushed toward her.

No one had heard a gunshot.

Lawrence Collette Million, an 18-year-old recent graduate of New Utrecht High School—Fort Hamilton High School wouldn't open for another four years, and Bay Ridge High School wasn't coed—lived at 6809 Third Avenue, above a grocery store, where he worked as an errand boy. Million dreamed, he later said, of becoming an expert in ballistics. (It had been a field of study since at least the nineteenth century, but just the year before, ballistics evidence had been used to clear police involvement in the St. Valentine's Day Massacre in Chicago, leading to the creation of that city's first crime-detection laboratory and the popularization of the science.)

Million, who called himself Larry, spent the afternoon of Sunday, June 13, with seven of his friends in Coney Island, most of it at a shooting gallery. There, Million pocketed a cartridge, a .22; he had bought a rifle of that caliber two weeks earlier, for $3 [*roughly $50, adjusted for inflation*]. He also owned two pistols, a derringer and a double-barrel, the kind gamblers used in the Old West.

He ended that Sunday up on his roof, pointing his .22-caliber rifle, loaded with the Coney Island bullet, at the electric lights of the Bay Ridge Theater, about a thousand feet away. He wanted to test the range of his new gun.

He aimed five feet above the marquee.

The bullet had entered Dorothy Carlucci's body under the left shoulder blade, went through her left lung and her heart and stopped in the membrane around her right lung. The medical examiner at Kings County Hospital said it had been fired levelly and not from a nearby rooftop—probably not imagining it could have come from a rooftop four blocks away.

Dorothy had been arm-in-arm with her husband and sister when hit; she collapsed to the ground. "I'm shot, Gene!" she screamed. Patrolman Lofrisco picked her up off Third Avenue and took her back inside the movie theater, to the manager's office, and a doctor was summoned from Norwegian Hospital (a precursor to Lutheran, then on 46th and Fourth). Almost two thousand people were still inside the theater, unaware that a woman was dying in another room.

Dorothy Carlucci would be carried out in a bodybag, according to photos that later ran in *Life*. She was 39.

Dozens of police officers were quickly engaged, but investigators were baffled. No one saw anyone running from the scene. No one had heard the shot. At 6 a.m., police began searching nearby roofs and cellars but turned up no weapons or clues. The victim's husband, Gene, insisted he had no enemies, even though he owned a trucking business on Renwick Street, in Manhattan, near the Holland Tunnel; he hadn't even been called to testify in a recent, high-profile trucking-racket investigation.

"How am I ever going to break it to him?" Gene kept saying. "The poor kid, the poor kid." He was talking about their son, Eugene Jr., 20, who studied agriculture at Cornell.

Despite the medical examiner's report, the initial theory was that someone had been shooting at the marquee lights; tenants of a nearby apartment house recalled two boys "taking pot shots with a rifle from the roof," the *Eagle* reported, and a tailor with a storefront at 7217 Third Avenue said that, a year earlier, a shop window had been smashed that way.

The questioning of neighborhood boys led investigators to Million. After firing, he had seen the crowd, rushed downstairs and learned what had happened from three friends, who'd been near the theater to see the shot. His friends promised "they wouldn't give [him] over," he later told police.

But it took less than a day for police to arrest him. Million wore "a well-worn pair of dungarees and a shirt without a necktie," the *Eagle* reported. "When he appeared at the lineup his wavy brown hair and boyish appearance was a distinct departure from the usual types."

The police who interrogated him reportedly liked him, or at least appreciated his frankness and sincerity. "The youth never shed a tear during his entire ordeal," the *Eagle* reported, "but it appeared to be the tearlessness of the deepest grief."

Such sympathy for Million pervaded much of the *Eagle*'s coverage. Less than a week after the shooting, the paper ran an item about the boy's mother, Marie (also, like Dorothy, married to a Eugene, though hers had died), who had a heart condition and had collapsed when she heard the news about her son. She attended Dorothy's funeral and announced that the new widower had told her he would not press homicide charges; that he would "offer sufficient aid to make it unnecessary for me to hire an expensive attorney"; and he would "do what he can to obtain [Larry Million's] freedom."

Larry was held at Raymond Street. His mother tried to raise the $10,000 bail [*more than $170,000, adjusted for inflation*], even though he had told her not to. "This has always been a respectable family, and I've never gone through anything like this," she told the *Eagle*. "Oh, how I hope to God this thing had never happened!" A few days later, Larry's old boss at the grocery story said he would rehire him.

"There seems to be a lot of misplaced sympathy for Lawrence Million," A LAW-ABIDING CITIZEN wrote to the *Eagle* that July. "But what about Mrs. Carlucci's relatives? I haven't seen or heard any sympathy expressed for them.

"I do hope this boy gets the limit of the law. What earthly right did he have to be shooting out electric lights on a theater? Electric signs are private property, and he is old enough to respect the rights of others."

*

On June 30, Million was indicted on charges of first-degree manslaughter, and his bail was lowered to $1,000. Almost five months later to the day, on Monday, November 29, just four days after Thanksgiving, Million pleaded guilty to second-degree manslaughter, likely the result of a deal.

When Marie heard he'd pleaded guilty, she had to be led from the courtroom, screaming.

Two weeks later he was sentenced. The defense asked for leniency. Larry had a good reputation. If he were sent to jail, it would devastate his widowed, hardworking mother. Plus, "the specter of the tragedy is always before Lawrence. He has repeatedly told me so. He is remorseful, repentant. The shooting was entirely accidental. The pangs of conscience he will always suffer should be punishment enough."

"You have drawn a pathetic picture of the family," the judge said. "But...the death of Mrs. Carlucci was caused by malicious conduct. The defendant admits he was firing at bulbs at the theater, and that act alone constituted a violation of the law in utter disregard of the rights of others."

He sentenced Million to an indefinite term in the New York Vocational Institution, in West Coxsackie, New York, a sort of postjuvenile reformatory.

Lawrence Million turns up just once more in the Brooklyn *Eagle* archives, almost seven years after his sentencing—on August 9, 1944. He has lost the haunted,

82

wounded look he so often possessed in photos at the time of the shooting; his face is fuller, older, and his hair looks shaggy.

It's in a column, "From Overseas." Million had been across the ocean since May of that year. There's no mention of his crime, or of whether he was released to fight in the war or if he had been released earlier—just the news that he had received the Air Medal in England.

Million had joined the Air Force, as a tail gunner.

8

Christina Oliveri and Nino Columbo

James Hawkes took his terrier, Spot, for a walk. It was February 6, 1938, a cloudy Sunday, and it had either just stopped raining or was about to start. Hawkes lived at 9203 Third Avenue, long since torn down. Despite the weather, the 15-year-old planned to walk almost a mile; he made it three thousand feet before his plans changed.

He very likely headed down 92nd Street—past Ridge, past Colonial, to Shore Road, where he turned left and came back up Oliver Street. There, alongside 9269 Shore Road, what the newspapers later called a "fashionable" apartment building, he "noticed [a] woman's stockingless leg sticking out from the rear door" of a two-door Pontiac sedan parked at the curb, the Buffalo *Courier Express* reported. He peeked inside—and saw two corpses in the backseat. He ran into the building and told an employee, who phoned the police.

The dead were Nino Columbo, 42, and Christina Oliveri, 24, both whom were married—but not to each other. Oliveri was found "lying on her side," the *Times* reported. Columbo was "hunched over her on his knees. Both were bruised and bloodstained. The bodies had been covered with an oblong piece of pale green oil cloth, figured profusely with tiny identical dancing couples." (Police thought this unique item might be their best clue, but it doesn't seem that anything came of it.)

85

> The woman...wore a black dress beneath
> a green overcoat with a fur collar. A false
> diamond pin was at the bodice. Her wed-
> ding ring had not been disturbed. She had
> no hat, and a pair of black pumps lay on
> the floor.

Her coat "was half off and jammed in the closed door of the car," the *Courier Express* continued, "as though she had fought to escape when she became aware of her captors' murderous intentions. Scratches on both indicated they battled to escape their fate. In addition, the rear seat had been wrenched from its place and had partly fallen over the bodies.

"The woman...was nude from the waist down."

Around their throats were the sash cords that had been used to strangle them, old clothesline tied in sailor's knots, "wound tightly three times around the necks of each," the *Eagle* reported.

Both had been dead for nine days.

Columbo lived at 2305 E. 4th Street, in Gravesend, with his wife, Catherine, and their children, Joseph and Loretta. In the last decade, Columbo had been arrested ten times and convicted twice—he went to Elmira Prison in 1916, for robbery, and to Sing Sing in 1920, for burglary. He was a "two-bit hoodlum," according to *The Great Pictorial History of World Crime, Volume 2*, by Jay Robert Nash. He "had been born in Brazil of Italian parents and had immigrated to the U.S. at an early age, and, throughout the 1920s and 1930s, he lived through robbery and extortion, loaning out his services to any New York mob seeking strong-arm enforcers." His son, Joseph, who "showed no remorse" over his father's death, eventually became the head of the Profaci crime family. (An assassination attempt in 1971 left him in a coma for seven years before he died.)

Two years before his murder, Nino's most recent arrest had been for vagrancy. By the time he was killed, he was known, the *Times* reported, as "a dealer in cheeses and oils" who spent most of his free time at the Dyker Heights golf course, where his friends were primarily women. Many papers referred to him as an "amateur golfer." A set of golf clubs was found in the Pontiac with the bodies. "The dress worn by the dead woman was part of a sports outfit," the *Eagle* reported.

Oliveri lived at 1745 74th Street, in Bensonhurst, with her husband, Alfred, and their sons, Frank and Joseph. Alfred had been on welfare since health problems had stopped him from working, as an embroiderer. He told police he didn't know Nino, but "she had mentioned a flirtatious man named Tony, whose face she had threatened to slap," the *Times* reported.

She was last seen by her husband on Friday; she'd told him she was going to the movies. When she didn't come home, Alfred reported her missing, dropped the kids off at his mother-in-law's on Stillwell Avenue and moved in with his brothers in the Bronx. Columbo was also last seen on Friday, alone, at a bar-and-grill at 7324 Eighteenth Avenue.

Some investigators believed they'd been murdered that night, kept somewhere for more than a week, then moved nine days later, in thick fog, to the spot on Oliver Street. (Unless the car had been there for days? No one seemed sure; eighteen cops—a dozen patrolmen and half a dozen sergeants—were charged with neglect of duty for failing to have found the car sooner, especially because two days before the bodies were found police had ticketed a nearby car on Oliver Street for parking overnight, which was illegal then, if not always enforced. It's not clear if the officers were ever punished.)

"I figured he had been picked up by you guys when he didn't come home," Columbo's wife told police, according to the website Mafia Genius. It wasn't unusual for him to disappear for days at a time, she said, though she didn't know about affairs with other women. "Brought into the police garage, Mrs. Columbo was shown her husband's blood covered face," the *Eagle* reported. "She took one quick look, cried, 'That's him!' and fainted." She described their marriage as happy.

A simple funeral service was held for Christina Oliveri on February 9, 1938, at Our Lady of Grace on Avenue W, near Columbo's house. Her widower carried in their youngest son while the eldest walked alongside him. After mass, the funeral procession passed Columbo's home, where family told reporters Columbo would likely be given a funeral two days later—but not at OLG, the pastor said. ("Priest Forbids Rites to Man in Double Murder," read the headline in the *Eagle*.)

Oliveri was buried at St. John's Cemetery, in Middle Village, Queens—the same plot where her oldest son, Frank, was buried in 2006. (The same cemetery where Florence McVey and Nora Kelly, from Chapter 6, were buried three years earlier; and Victoria Muspratt, from Chapter 5; and Vannie Higgins, from Chapter 3.)

Columbo had been a loanshark, the "most stubborn rival" of Cassendro "Anthony" "The Chief" Bonasera, "strong-arm ruler of Brooklyn's shylock racket since the death of Frankie Yale," or Uale, in 1928, the *Eagle* reported. Oliveri had just been with the wrong man at the wrong time. (As the *Eagle* had put it the day after the bodies were discovered, "Columbo was apparently murdered by business enemies and the woman killed to silence her.") Robbery wasn't a motive; Columbo had $13 on him [*more than $230, adjusted for inflation*].

Gunmen had once tried to assassinate Bonasera, a Dyker Heights resident who always gave his address as 7515 Thirteenth Avenue; in 1930 he was shot in the head, neck and arm. He survived. By 1939, Bonasera was wanted for questioning in Columbo's and Oliveri's murders, as was his lieutenant John Oddo, also known as Johnny Bath Beach. The two were close; Oddo had been the best man at Bonasera's wedding. They were like usual suspects out of Central Casting, rounded up when the police needed to look busy. They were arrested often but convicted rarely, and never for serious offenses.

Oddo was picked up near 81st and Columbus in Manhattan in May 1939 on extortion charges. His bail was set at $100,000 [*almost $1.8 million, adjusted for inflation*], which was lowered to $50,000 on appeal and then, two months later, during which time he'd languished in the Tombs, to $25,000, "which the District Attorney's office said it did not oppose," the *Eagle* reported, "with the understanding that Oddo would supply information to the police which would help them to catch up with" Bonasera and another lieutenant.

It's unclear if Oddo did supply such information; both men were eventually convicted of extortion and conspiracy, though neither seems to have served much time for it. Shortly thereafter the two had a falling out; in 1947, eight unsolved murders in Bath Beach were said to be from the war between Bonasera and Oddo's now-rival bookmaking factions; sixty detectives were deployed to stop the violence and bring the perpetrators to justice.

In 1953, the United States tried to deport Bonasera, following an arrest in Washington by the department of justice "on charges of engaging in commercialized vice and loan-sharking," the *Eagle* reported. At that point he had been arrested twenty-five times, but he had received only four minor convictions, and "only one could be construed as involving moral turpitude," the blog Buffalo Mob explains. "By law, two such convictions were required for deportation."

"Bonasera was sought for some time as a prime suspect in the underworld execution of [his former boss Frankie Yale] but never was officially charged with it," the *Eagle* added. "He was from time to time questioned about numerous other unsolved gang murders, which remained unsolved"—such as the long-forgotten deaths of Nino Columbo and Christina Oliveri.

Both Bonaera and Oddo died in the 1970s—of natural causes.

9

Margaret Jokiel

Before gunshots busted the front windows, lodging bullets into the living-room walls, the phone rang. Esther Jokiel was home on Wednesday evening, April 28, 1948, about 9 p.m., when she picked up. A voice she later described as high-pitched and soprano asked for her daughter, a math teacher at Fort Hamilton High School, opened just seven years earlier; but Margaret, a music lover, was at Carnegie Hall, at a performance of the Down Town Glee Club. (As a student at St. Joseph's, in Clinton Hill, she had been a member of the glee club. Apparently she liked glee clubs.) The caller hung up.

A few minutes later, the phone rang again. Esther, also a teacher, at P.S. 102, picked up the second floor extension. Her husband was in the bedroom, asleep. The same voice shouted, "Pass everyone in math or you'll be pushing up daisies!" Esther thought it was a practical joke, until she heard the gunfire. Twenty-eight bullets, from .22-caliber rifles stolen from a Coney Island shooting gallery, had been fired at the house, 127 98th Street, near the end of the dead-end block; seven got through one-and-a-half inches of front-door and into the living room.

Four more bullets went into neighbors' houses, Nos. 129 and 133. The former was home to a contractor named Eugene Reynolds, who was sitting in the dining room with his wife when a bullet came through a living room window; the latter was home to Professor John Horan, of St. John's University, who was sitting on his porch when his phone rang. As he went inside to answer it, "a bullet ripped into the wall directly in line with where his head had been," the Brooklyn *Eagle* reported.

The car from which the shots had been fired sped away, its headlights off. No one had been hurt. But Margaret was shaken. She called the incident "fantastic." Police guarded the house all night, and her uncle, a sergeant, escorted her to school the next morning, where she administered exams; defiantly, she told a reporter she would "fail those who do not receive passing grades." The principal, Dr. Ludwig, found a substitute by the end of the school day so Margaret could go home and "rest." He surmised the crime was "a lark of an adolescent with no thought to the consequences," or that the assailant was "just a wise guy."

Margaret Jokiel was "pretty, blond, 24 years old," according to the *Eagle*; later it called her "slim, attractive." In fact, all the reporting on the incident, including by the Associated Press, which turned the story into national news, made a point to mention her appearance. A headline in the Milwaukee *Journal* read, "Pretty Teacher Gives Exams Under Guard After Shots, Warning."

Police planned to question one hundred of her students about their whereabouts the previous evening. They went through ninety-six of them before they caught a break. A proctor covering for Miss Jokiel spotted a boy taking the algebra test who didn't belong there. That boy became confused when he was questioned; he had a Western Union money order made out to a name different from that of the student he was supposed to be.

That money order was payment to take the test for a fellow 16-year-old, so terrified of that test that he had lead the effort to scare his math teacher with gunfire. The night before, he'd roused some friends, all 14 or 15 years old, at a candy store on Fort Hamilton Parkway and 66th Street, left instructions with one to phone-in the threat at 9 p.m., and took another four to steal a car; they stopped at the ringleader's home to pick up seven stolen rifles and ammunition, covered the headlights and license plates with handkerchiefs, and, at about 9:30 p.m., fired.

The gang abandoned the stolen car and retired to a soda fountain, where the ringleader enlisted his substitute for the test. The next day, within four hours of discovering that ringer, several boys were in custody—five charged with discharging firearms in the city without a permit and the caller charged with acting in concert; the test taker was released by police but expected to face disciplinary action from the school. Another two boys were charged later.

The ringleader was held on $10,000 bail [*almost $100,000, adjusted for inflation*] at the Raymond Street Jail on a felony charge of malicious mischief—for causing $250 in damage. He was arraigned in Adolescent Court; the others were arraigned in Children's Court, charged with juvenile delinquency, of which they would eventually all be found guilty. One was placed on probation. Another was sent to live with his family in Elmont and attend school there; he was ordered "not to return to his old haunts"; the other five were sent to the State Training School for Boys in Warwick, New York.

The *Eagle* reported:

> Judge James V. Mulholland declared the responsibility for "the dangerous trend juvenile delinquency has progressively reached" is shared by parents, the Board of Education and other city authorities. He said the court could not excuse the defendants because of their youth, warning that would "increase the menace and leave the community at the mercy of irresponsible hoodlums and incipient gangsters."

Three of the boys, the ones who'd stolen the rifles, also confessed to having stolen microscopes, typewriters and movie projectors from Fort Hamilton High School; all were recovered. The *Eagle* never named any of the children, and it never reported what happened to the 16-year-old ringleader.

At the end of the year, *Eagle* readers voted this story the fourth-biggest news story of 1948, behind Marine Park and Jamaica Bay residents' ending odoriferous garbage dumping; the resignation of Leo Durocher, manager of the Dodgers; and the rape and murder of an 80-year-old woman in Bed-Stuy.

Within three weeks of the shooting, Margaret's father, Paul, died. The funeral was held at the bullet-scarred house. Esther died four years later, in June 1952; her funeral was also held at the house. In 1949, Miss

Jokiel got engaged to John Joyce, of 428 74th Street, and the following year they married, at St. Patrick's.

Miss Jokiel, by the way, had graded the ringer's test.
   He got a 43.

10

Helen Olsen

At about 2:30 a.m. on Friday, November 7, 1952, residents of 6823 Ridge Boulevard spilled out onto the street, huddling in their pajamas, even though it was 36 degrees outside with the wind chill; there was a fire in the building. After putting it out, firefighters followed the one-alarm blaze to its source—an apartment on the second floor—and broke down the door. They found Helen Olsen just inside, dead, in the foyer, "where she had apparently fallen after a desperate attempt to escape the blazing apartment," the Brooklyn *Eagle* reported.

"She lay, magnificent in death and naked as the day she was born, on the floor just inside her own doorsill," a magazine later reported, rather floridly. "Her outstretched arms told only too graphically how narrowly she had missed reaching the revivifying fresh air. How close she had been when the gaseous poison of the smoke filled her lungs and cut her down."

It looked like a routine accident, and it might have been written off as such, if a week later an anonymous tipster hadn't called the *Eagle*.

Look at the boyfriend, she'd said.

But first investigators had to figure out who her boyfriend was.

*

The *Eagle* waffled on the details about Olsen. One article calls her Helen Olsen Gjelland. The small item about the fire says her husband, a seaman, was away; all subsequent articles refer to her as a divorcée. The fullest account of her death I found comes from the May 1956 issue of *True Crime*, though its salacious headline—"Last Orgy of a Blond Barfly"—suggests its lurid details and novelistic dialogue might be exaggerated for maximum tawdriness. ("She liked her booze and she was just crazy about men," the subhed proclaims. "Too bad that she couldn't handle both at the same time!")

But Stephen R. Hoyt's reporting, if considered with skepticism, fills in many of the holes left in the cursory daily reporting. According to his piece, Olsen was *twice* divorced. She also "had everything a woman might reasonably want."

> She was tall, with the magnificently proportioned figure of a Viking goddess. She had a beautiful face crowned by a glory of natural golden hair. She had three lovely children and a man who was slavishly devoted to her.

> Yet Helen Olsen was desperately, unrelentingly unhappy. Her face and figure had led her to nothing but trouble. Her three children by her two divorced husbands had been taken away from her. The one man who really loved her—her fiancé—was away at sea most of the time. She had no choice, she felt, but to solace her-

self with lesser men, and with the whiskey
bottle.

Olsen was a well-known habituée of the local bars.
"There wasn't one that Helen had missed," *True Crime*
reported. "Drunk or sober, her radiant presence was like
a breath of fresh air in the murky barrooms of Bay
Ridge. Everyone knew her."

So detectives started canvassing them, hunting for
leads, because on closer inspection the fire didn't look
quite right—it had started in the closet, but Olsen hadn't
hung up her clothes; there were no matches or cigarette
butts in the bedroom; and there were two whiskey glasses in her kitchen but only one stained with lipstick. Soon
they found the woman who had called the *Eagle*. "It isn't
what the police think," she had told the paper. "*That
woman was deliberately set on fire*." (The Brooklyn *Eagle* not
only forwarded this tip to authorities but also sat on the
story so as not to disturb the investigation. "This is an
example of what an alert citizen, in co-operation with a
public-spirited newspaper, can do," the district attorney
said, adding thanks for "subordinating a news story to
the public good without fanfare.")

The woman tried to pin the arson on her boyfriend,
whom *True Crime* calls Larson (a fake name), because she
was jealous of the attention he paid to Olsen.

"Like many sections of New York, Bay Ridge is a
small, neighborly community within a large city," *True
Crime* reported. "Everybody knows everyone else—par-
ticularly in the taverns."

Helen Olsen had done a lot of drinking with Larson. When they were drunk he'd sometimes paw her. But Helen had drunk with many other men who did the same thing. As did Larson with other women. There was no evidence that Helen was Larson's special girl.

Police considered that the tipster might have done it; one time she had smashed a glass, picked up a shard and tried to cut Olsen's face. But she had an alibi—she was too wasted to kill anyone that night; she had been escorted home and put to bed by Chester Elliott, a long-distance truck driver. (She'd told police that her boyfriend Larson had once tried to light her nightgown on fire; when police asked Elliott what he thought of that story, he blushed. She never slept in a nightgown, he said—she always slept "raw.")

On a hunch, detectives checked out Elliott, 42, who lived in a furnished room in a brick rowhouse at 459 49th Street, and discovered that in the last twenty years, he'd been arrested five times, twice for disorderly conduct, twice for felonious assault and once for grand larceny. (Each case had been dismissed or the sentence suspended, so Elliott had never spent time in prison. Larson also had a few arrests, all for drunkenness.) Suspicious, they questioned him; he denied knowing Olsen, and said he'd gone straight home after putting the accuser to bed, but bartenders identified him as someone who had shared drinks with Olsen numerous times.

Apparently, he'd gone back out that night.

Detectives interrogated him again, and this time, he confessed. From *True Crime*:

> "I got up out of bed," he said. "Helen stayed there. She was very drunk.

> "I asked her for a date over the weekend. She told me that she couldn't go because she had a date with someone else. While I was getting dressed, she turned over facing the wall and fell asleep."

> That made him mad, Elliott said. And he was jealous of her other date. He lit a cigarette, stood looking down at her as he smoked, admiring her. And his jealousy, his terrible longing to possess her alone for himself, mounted till it became a frenzy of rage, a whiplash goading him to maniac fury.

> "The door of the clothes closet was open," he related, "so I threw the cigarette inside. I thought I'd fix her. I'd burn up her clothes so she couldn't keep her date with this other guy." Then he walked into the kitchen, he said, and downed a drink of Scotch.

> "I sat there about 20 minutes drinking whiskey," he continued. "I saw a slight haze of smoke, but didn't do anything about it. I had four or five more drinks."

Then he heard the roar of flames. A huge
ball of fire leaped from the clothes closet.
He said, "I took my topcoat from the
kitchen and ran out of the apartment.

"I guess I just blew my top."

Elliott was booked at 3:30 a.m. on Saturday, November
22, fifteen days after Olsen had died, almost to the hour.
And on May 28, 1953, he pleaded guilty to first-degree
manslaughter (rather than risk a trial for first-degree
murder). That July, he was sentenced to seven-to-fifteen
in Sing Sing—all because of an anonymous phone call to
a newspaper that hadn't even been about him.

11

Patsy Hylan and Dorothy Cameron
(all names have been changed)

On Wednesday evening, April 17, 1957, Helen Marino was walking home from a friend's house. It was dark, and drizzling, as she traveled the one block down Marine Avenue, toward 94th Street, where she lived. She heard moaning. As she reached the corner, a green sedan came speeding up 94th, hooked a right on Marine and disappeared. Marino turned down her block, toward the shore, the way the car had come, and the moaning got louder. She saw something across the road—half on the sidewalk, half in the street.

When she realized it was a person, she ran inside and called the police.

Officers from the 64th Precinct responded within minutes. The location was just two hundred seconds by car from the old station house, on 86th and Fourth. The patrolmen were looking for No. 52, which Marino had specified, but they stopped instead a few doors past it, in front of No. 58, a one-family A-frame attached on its west-side to another just like it. It was just before midnight.

The police saw it, too: a woman, lying with her head on the curb and her legs in the road. The block was dark, its only streetlight about 100 feet away from the woman, but the patrol car's headlights lit up the scene.

Her face looked toward the bay; her feet pointed inland. She wore a single pink glove. Her black mouton coat was open, revealing a light-blue wool dress pushed up above her waist, perhaps as high as her chest; she wasn't wearing shoes or underwear—not even stockings. Her underpants and girdle were looped loosely around her left ankle. One of the officers tried to pull her coat closed.

She showed signs of life: her knees moved up and down, and she would bend her arms; the officer tried to hold down her hand, to stop it from touching her face, which was covered in blood. Dried blood caked under her hair, and her forehead looked like it had been pushed in. Her left ear was barely hanging on. Her face was black-and-blue, and multiple cuts went down so deep you could touch bone. Brain tissue escaped from above her eyes. She moaned. Cops said she looked like she was trying to sit up, but she couldn't. Two officers held her down by the shoulders.

The woman—gray-eyed, five-foot-six, 115 pounds—couldn't answer questions, and the patrolmen used their radio car to call for an ambulance and for their sergeant. One patrolman remained on the scene while another sped to 89th Street and Colonial Road, about five blocks away, to the nearest call box they knew of, to notify the precinct and request detectives. More patrolmen arrived, as did the detectives, a sergeant, and an assistant DA. One patrolman retrieved a doctor from his home at 121 Marine Avenue, about a block away. The sergeant sent another to fetch the nearest Catholic priest, assuming the woman was Catholic.

It had been raining earlier, and the street was wet, but now it just drizzled. The doctor thought a heated foyer would be a better spot for the woman than the damp street, so, about twenty minutes after the first responders had arrived, two officers put her body on a stretcher and moved it to the Shore Road Nursing Home, which no longer exists but then could accommodate twenty-five people on the several lots it occupied a few doors down. In the lobby, the doctor checked her pulse and got nothing; her skin was cold. He and a nurse washed some blood from her head and put a sterile dressing over the wound; it required several four-by-four pieces of gauze just to cover it, to keep out dirt. She seemed to moan when they removed her turban, but when a priest spoke to her, she didn't respond.

There wasn't much else to do but wait for the ambulance, which would bring her to Coney Island Hospital. A nurse there described her as kicking, screaming and incoherent. They had to cut her dress off because of the damage to her head. She was bleeding profusely and in shock. Doctors couldn't find a pulse; she barely had any blood pressure, and she was barely breathing. They jammed a shot of adrenaline into her heart; it did nothing. They cut open her chest and massaged her heart with their hands; it kept her alive for five or ten more minutes. They put her in an iron lung; it gave her another five minutes. She wasn't pronounced dead until 3:30 a.m.

Patricia Hylan was 19 years old.

And his second victim.

*

Tommy Hutchins was 22 years old, six-foot-two, blond, husky, lumpen-faced. He lived with two sisters and their parents on the third floor of the apartment building on the southwest corner of 78th and Third, though he wouldn't for long: he was engaged to a blonde from the neighborhood, and the wedding was set for May 11 at the family's parish, Our Lady of Angels. She lived at 340 Ovington Avenue, the end of a series of midblock rowhouses.

On Saturday, April 20, exactly three weeks before the wedding day, detectives dropped in at the apartment on 78th Street. They were looking for Hutchins, who wasn't there. For the past seven months, Hutchins had been working six blocks away, on Third Avenue near 72nd Street—up the block from P.S. 102, the elementary school he'd graduated from at the age of 15—doing service and installations for a firm that dealt in coal, oil burners and heating equipment and operated out of the Bay Ridge Theater building, outside which Dorothy Carlucci had been shot in 1937 (see Chapter 7). Hutchins made $65 a week [*approximately $575, adjusted for inflation*]—sometimes, with overtime, as much as $75.

Detectives found Hutchins at his job around noon and asked him if they could see his car. Hutchins drove a green sedan, a two-door 1955 Ford, license plate KB 8602, registered to his boss. Hutchins used the car for service calls—when police found it, there was a toolbox on the floor in the backseat—but he had permission to use it for personal affairs, as well, because he would sometimes need it to make emergency calls. Hutchins told detectives it was parked around the corner. As the three walked to the car, Hutchins broke the silence.

"I might as well tell you. The car is messed up."

"What do you mean, 'The car is messed up'?"

Hutchins told them it was full of blood.

Three days earlier, on April 17, the day Patsy Hylan was killed, Tommy Hutchins had installed an oil burner at 171 15th Street. He kicked off as usual at 5 p.m. and half an hour later had dropped into the Melody Room, a bar across the street from his office, once a favorite of local novelists Hubert Selby, Jr., and Gilbert Sorrentino. Hutchins sat at the bar and drank three or four beers over the next two hours; these were short beers, five ounces, maybe four if they had a head, costing 15 cents apiece [*$1.30, adjusted for inflation*]. He accompanied each with a shot of Seagram's 7. He didn't order any of the pretreated sandwiches the bar offered, even though he hadn't eaten anything since a sandwich at lunch, around 11 a.m.

His fiancée was out shopping for their upcoming wedding, he later testified. Hutchins had $120 in his pocket, in case he needed to put down a deposit for an apartment for the two of them.

His closest friend, James Warner—whose brother was married to one of Hutchins's sisters—showed up at 7 p.m. with his girlfriend, Lynn. Their friend Larry came in, maybe half an hour later. Hutchins drank probably eight more short beers. He played a guessing game with the other customers involving fistfuls of matches. He chatted with the bartender about baseball and joked about getting married soon. "You must be getting bad now," the bartender chided him. "You're starting to count the days left."

Hutchins bought a belt or two from a partially blind boy who made his living selling belts from tavern to tavern; he also bought a set of cufflinks and tie clasp from a woman who came in hawking clothes and costume jewelry. Larry had spent almost an hour in the bar's phone booth, and when he came out he gathered James, Lynn and Hutchins for a trip downtown to a cabaret where you could dance to a live band. They left the Melody Room about 9 p.m. Hutchins wasn't drunk, Warner later testified. "I'd say he was feeling good, though."

"Would you say he was feeling very high?" the defense attorney asked at the murder trial.

"I would."

The group piled into Hutchins's car, which was parked 100 feet away, near Ovington Avenue, where his fiancée lived. After a few errands, Hutchins took the streets, stopping for red lights along the way, to the Park Terrace Bar & Grill, on Park Place and Flatbush. But Hutchins and Warner couldn't get served at the bar, because they weren't properly dressed. Hutchins was still in his workclothes: denim jacket, whipcord trousers and a checked flannel shirt; his buddy had a jacket but no tie.

The group split up. Lynn had friends inside; she went in with Larry while Hutchins and James went into a cabaret across the street for twenty minutes and drank three or four whiskeys each, before James went back to the Park Terrace to get Lynn. They had a fight, and she got in a cab back to Bay Ridge. Hutchins, at this point, was "very 'high,'" Warner testified, but he still drove the other two boys home. He drove James to Lynn's place on 20th Street (not James's own place, 7223 Fourth Avenue), then took the highway at Prospect Avenue, got off around Owl's Head Park, and dropped Larry at his place, 7504 Third Avenue.

Then Hutchins went back to the Melody Room.

Leon Hylan, Jr., identified his sister's body on the afternoon of April 18, hours after she'd died in Coney Island Hospital. The 28-year-old worked as a patrolman in Manhattan. His father, Leon, Sr., twenty years older, was a packer at a chewing gum plant. Junior cried when he saw Patsy's ring. "I gave it to her myself," he said. Leon lived with his brown-haired sister and their parents at 552 73rd Street, the keys to which, recovered from the victim, Junior also identified: the long one for the front door of the building, the short one for the front door of the apartment, on a ring, decorated with charms, that Leon had bought Patsy a few years ago for her birthday.

He was relieved of his routine duties after his sister's murder so he could assist in the investigation.

The following Saturday, April 20, Hutchins and the two detectives walked to Hutchins's car, parked in front of 251 72nd Street, a handsome rowhouse, still standing, with a slanted roof and bay windows. When Hutchins unlocked the door, a detective noted the car had new seat covers—green, with white and yellow stripes, which

Hutchins had bought the previous day at Strauss, the department store on Senator and Fourth—over the front and back seats, which were indeed stained: dark stains, brownish, or a deep red, mostly on the passenger side of the vehicle, in the front seat and the back, on the floor, in the cracks in the floor.

Hutchins told them that on Wednesday night, the night Patsy Hylan turned up on a curb with seventeen skull fractures, his car had been stolen, even though he had locked it. He was drinking at the Melody Room, came out around 8 or 9 p.m. and found his car missing, so went back and had a few more drinks, and came back out at midnight to find it returned, the windows locked, the car full of blood.

The detectives brought Hutchins to the station—in his own car, because they'd walked there. Hutchins rode in the front seat, on the passenger side.

The detectives parked out front, and other officers then moved it to the station garage, where a third detective had it photographed and removed various objects and articles: a pair of workman's coveralls from the backseat, the stains on the legs of which would later test positive for blood; a screwdriver from the glove compartment, whose handle also tested positive; and a cardboard box of tools from the trunk, including a ball-peen hammer, all of which tested positive, too. So did the backseat of the car. And the workclothes he was wearing when he was taken into custody. Another detective found a woman's purse under the driver's seat.

That afternoon, the Hylans were at Joseph Redmond's, a funeral parlor at 476 73rd Street, down the block from their home, making arrangements for Patsy.

On her last night, Patsy Hylan went out. She sometimes went to bars on weekends, at least that's what some of Tommy's friends later testified, but this was a Wednesday; she left her home about 8:30 p.m., the same time Hutchins was heading downtown, to go shopping, perhaps for an Easter hat, she'd told her mother. Easter was especially late that year. Then she walked to an ice-cream parlor, Joe and Howard's, half a block south of the Melody Room, on the west side of Third Avenue, No. 7208, which was her regular hangout.

She spotted a few friends, guys, who were having coffee in a booth in the middle of the store, and she joined them for half an hour, maybe less. When she left, she stayed outside to talk with a girlfriend, then stood by herself in front of the candy store on the corner of 72nd Street. Half a dozen acquaintances saw her outside; some saw her leaning against the front fender of a car, others as she crossed Third Avenue and walked up 72nd Street, toward Fourth Avenue.

"She was choosy about her friends," a deputy chief inspector told the Associated Press a few days later. "She did not drink. She was clean living. Her relatives and friends insisted that she was not the kind of a girl who would accept a ride from a stranger." The same article describes her dead body as fully dressed.

She disappeared from view of those on Third Avenue as she passed the building on the corner.

That's where Hutchins caught up with her.

Upstairs at the station house, Hutchins was brought into the squad commander's office, where about seven detectives, inspectors, captains, and lieutenants had gathered. No one read him his rights; *Miranda* v. *Arizona* would not be adjudicated for almost a decade.

An inspector asked Hutchins to explain the blood, which he couldn't. "I am not going to kid you," the inspector told him, according to his testimony at trial. "You are in on something serious, but you might as well tell the truth, because you are not going to improve your position by making us to go through a lot of checks all day, and taking hours to do something we can do in minutes.

"Now, that blood on your car has to be explained. Did you kill this girl?"

"Yes," Hutchins said, "I did."

The conversation had lasted about six minutes. Hutchins also admitted that he had killed before. He also said he had assaulted nine others, two of whom were immediately brought to the station and identified him.

News of the arrest worked its way through the neighborhood, and locals began to gather at the old precinct house on 86th Street. Police had to erect barricades to keep them on the sidewalks across the street. At least five hundred people turned up; some estimated that the crowd numbered three thousand.

*

Hutchins stayed at the Melody Room for half an hour, long enough to drink two beers. He left about 10:30 p.m., got in his car, which he'd parked near a taxi stand on the south side of 72nd Street, and was waiting for the light at Third Avenue when he saw Hylan cross the intersection. When the light changed, he caught up to her just past the avenue, opened the passenger-side door and asked if she wanted a ride. She did. Her foot was sore; she'd taken the day off from work at her job as a filing clerk at an insurance company near Columbus Circle.

Hutchins knew Hylan from seeing her around the Melody Room the last two months. In the car, she talked about her sore foot. He stopped around the corner from her parents' place, on Sixth Avenue. They sat in the car and talked. Then they started necking, Hutchins said.

But the block was too bright, so Hutchins drove her down 73rd Street, past Third Avenue, where it starts to get quieter, and stopped close to Ridge Boulevard, near the library and Episcopal church. They resumed necking. "I thought like she was going to give out," Hutchins later told police. She got out of the car, pushed the seat forward, and got into the backseat. Hutchins climbed back there too. She might have taken her underpants off. But every time he tried to take it to the next level, she said, "Not yet." She wanted a few drinks first. She wanted to go to the Melody Room.

Hutchins didn't. "Later," he told her. He sat back. She pulled away, then moved toward him again, put her arms around him, kissed him. He put his left hand above her knee, on her thigh. They kissed some more, and she told him, "Not yet." They kissed some more, and she told him, again, "Not yet." She'd been in his car almost twenty minutes.

There was a hammer nearby on the floor, a ball-peen hammer; it weighed about ten ounces, had about a twelve-inch handle. He grabbed it. He didn't say anything; he just hit her, a few times, at least. He didn't know how many times. "I blew my top," he later told police. "I went nuts." But he also said he wasn't angry. "It was a feeling that got over me," he said. "I started to shake."

The medical examiner testified he hit her at least nineteen times.

Then he climbed back into the front seat and drove. He drove all the way to some block in the 90s, one he didn't know, then stopped, dragged her out of the car, and laid her out in the street, with her head on the curb. Then he drove home on Third Avenue, parked his car at about 1 a.m., went upstairs and got six hours of sleep.

In the morning, he tossed her handbag and her shoes in somebody's garbage can on Third Avenue, at 71st Street, or close to it. (Dozens of sanitation workers and detectives would later search through tons of trash on Staten Island looking for them.) Then he went to work. After his shift, Hutchins went to Strauss and bought new seat covers, and then he went to see his fiancée. He put the seat covers on the next morning, Friday, the day before police would visit him at work.

(During trial, the defense briefly but vigorously cross-examined a detective who'd spent seventy-five minutes alone with Hutchins when he was brought in for questioning—and implied he told Hutchins to lie, to say the

girl had resisted him, in order at least to save her character; Hutchins would testify to this at length. The detective denied it. This might explain why Hutchins, in a second interview immediately after the first, after a coffee
break unrecorded by the stenographer, told police he
was the one who took her underpants off, which made
her scream, and that he hit her so she would stop
screaming, and also so she couldn't tell anyone what he
had done. "I was angry," he said this time, even though
he'd just said the opposite.)

Hutchins wasn't impotent. He hadn't raped her. He
got no sexual satisfaction from hitting her. He hadn't
spent time in any mental institutions. He hadn't even
been arrested before. He didn't know why he had hit
her, he said.

But she wasn't the first person he'd hurt.

A close friend of Hylan told the UP that Hutchins had
been stalking his victim since February and had tried to
attack her as many as four times as she walked home
after dark; he would emerge from dark alleys and try to
grab her, but she would scream and scare him off. They
never told her family because they didn't want to worry
them. (If this were true, it would cast doubt on Hutchins's story; why would she have gotten into his car?)

After his arrest, multiple women identified Hutchins
as their attacker, and several accused him of attempted
rape. Cops had been aware of this local menace. "Because the element of beating—usually about the face—
was always present, police...named him The Slapper,"
according to the *Home Reporter*.

One 40-year-old woman said he had broken her nose during a purse-snatching that netted Hutchins $85; when police showed him to her, she said, "That's the beast that hit me!" and police had to hold her back. (It was her purse detectives had found in Hutchins's car.) Two teenagers accused him of trying to rape them during a week in April. The latter said a tall, blond man had attempted, three blocks from Hylan's home, to drag her off the street at 2:10 a.m. into his green sedan—descriptions that matched Hutchins and his car—but gave up during a struggle.

Police were searching for such a suspect when they received a tip from James Dolan, a 33-year-old bank teller known as Buddy who lived in the same building as Hutchins, on 78th Street. Dolan described Hutchins as "a nervous, shifty fellow with something on his mind"; he knew Tommy was the man police wanted as soon as he read the suspect's description in the newspaper. An ex-Marine rejected from the police force for a service-connected ulcer operation he'd once undergone, Dolan told the Chicago *Tribune* it was a difficult decision: he'd known Hutchins since Hutchins was 10 years old, and they'd played on the same Catholic Youth Organization basketball team. "But when you come down to it," Dolan said, "what you care about are those you love. I'm thankful he's out of circulation.

"God knows who might have been next."

On May 4, Hutchins was indicted for a second murder, to which he had also confessed at his interrogation: the January 29 killing of Dorothy Cameron, a 53-year-old

116

divorcée. The cases were similar: Cameron lived at Flagg Court, the immense apartment complex whose main entrance, on Ridge Boulevard, is just half a block from where Hutchins had beaten Hylan with a hammer. Cameron, an administrative assistant at an aluminum company on Park Avenue, had met Hutchins in a bar and offered him a ride; it was cold that night, and had even snowed a little. They were parked near Flagg Court when they started making out. When Cameron resisted full sexual intercourse, Hutchins beat her with a pair of pliers.

Her 22-year-old daughter, who lived with her at Flagg Court, had reported her missing. A concerned patrolman cruised the neighborhood while off-duty, looking for Cameron's car; he found it after two days, in front of 66 73rd Street, not far from Narrows Avenue, with Cameron in the backseat. "Her skull had been fractured in six places," the Brooklyn *Spectator* reported, "and her face was crushed almost beyond recognition." Her purse, with $22 [*almost $200, adjusted for inflation*], was on the front seat, and she was still wearing her watch and her rings.

A local police lieutenant called the case a mystery— "the first mystery murder in Bay Ridge in more than 15 years," he told the *Spectator*. Fourteen detectives were assigned. Investigators eventually suspected Cameron's daughter's boyfriend, Russell Anderson, in her death, and the young couple complained of harassment by investigators—what the *Times* called "brutality and 'brainwashing.'" "At one point," according to the *Home Reporter*, "police shoved [the daughter] and knocked her glasses off and refused to let her see a lawyer." But the two were cleared of suspicion after Hutchins's confession, even though the daughter had also confessed to her mother's murder. Blond like Hutchins, and just an inch shorter and thirty pounds lighter, Anderson apparently could have passed for the killer's brother. The woman whose nose Hutchins had broken identified Anderson as her assailant, but recanted when Hutchins was arrested.

"Coincidentally, Anderson said he met Hutchins in a bar once two years ago," the Associated Press reported. "'He seemed like a very nice guy,' Anderson added."

Hutchins spent the night after his arrest at the station house, and for Easter breakfast he was served an egg sandwich and coffee before he was transported to police headquarters and then to Brooklyn Felony Court. A hundred people gathered outside when Hutchins was indicted for Hylan's murder, fewer than twenty-four hours after he'd confessed, and a dozen policemen were on hand to keep order. "It was feared that residents of the Fort Hamilton district, who had been incensed by the murders, might cause trouble," the *Times* reported. "None developed."

Inside, the judge excoriated Hutchins. "Of...the most gruesome crimes conjured in a girl's hideous dreams," he said, "you are charged with the most macabre." The judge ordered Hutchins held without bail and set a hearing for Tuesday—the same day Hylan's funeral mass would be sung to eighteen-hundred mourners (with another three-hundred outside) at Our Lady of Angels, the church where Hutchins was supposed to get married in a few weeks. His fiancée sat in the back of the courtroom and made no sound.

He was placed under twenty-four-hour guard, and they confiscated his belt—possibly one he'd purchased from the partially blind boy on the night of the murder.

Hutchins had confessed because police "pounded and pounded away at him and he just couldn't take it," his sister Catherine later told United Press. "There was no physical beating, but he is a nervous kid." The crime was picked up by papers around the country, and most depicted Hutchins as a remorseless fiend. But *Stars and Stripes* ran an article from the International News Service syndicate whose headline called him a "Perfect Gentleman."

"Hutchins...was regarded as a quiet, hardworking 'perfect gentleman' in the area. Informed of his confession, his father cried out, 'Oh, my God, no. Not Tommy! It can't be—he's a good boy.'" A friend described him at trial as "a very quiet-mannered type of person; well respected." He had no criminal record. "As far as the Hylan girl is concerned," Catherine told the AP, "his mind is a complete blank." She added Thomas "couldn't be in his right mind to do the things they said he did."

In May, weeks after a judge had thrown out his lawyer's previous insanity plea, Hutchins again pleaded not guilty to both murders, but not because he didn't commit them. He claimed insanity—specifically, by reason of epilepsy, which he said sometimes caused him to become violent and left him suffering from memory loss. He said he didn't remember anything between Hylan's saying

119

"not yet" and a blaring car horn alerting him that he was driving on the wrong side of the road. When he turned back to watch the passing car that had honked at him, he saw Hylan in the backseat, and figured he ought to drop her off some place. Say, on 94th Street.

"He was always mentally all right," Hutchins's father told the *Times*, "but when he came from the Army he told us he had some sort of neurological treatment in Japan. He told us they had operated on his brain, and I think it had something to do with pressure on his brain. I'm not sure whether he got a medical discharge."

Hutchins had served in the U.S. Army from May 1954 to June 1956, just after the Korean War, and during this time had been treated at neurological clinics in Japan, which had X-rayed his head when he complained of blackouts and seizures. Hutchins also got into trouble overseas, though it's unclear if he blamed his epilepsy: the AP reported in April 1957 that the Army had disclosed that Hutchins had been convicted in a court-martial of assaulting a Japanese girl while serving in Japan; he had been fined and demoted.

Hutchins's epilepsy had long been a problem—as many people in the neighborhood were well aware.

One of the last people to see Hylan alive was also a friend of Hutchins, and this man testified he had seen Hutchins have fits before, like four years before the murder, at an Our Lady of Angels parish dance, in August 1953. "He was swinging his hands and acting, like, you know, he just cracked up. You know what I mean," Jerome Jones testified.

"Strike that out," the judge said. "You saw him swinging his hands? … Show the jury how."

"Just going wild," Jones said.

Hutchins met up with his friend Jack Rogers about 7 p.m. the night of that dance. They didn't eat anything—they just drank beers, as many as fifteen six-ounce beers, at the Melody Room with a few other friends until they headed up to the church, around 8:30 p.m. Shortly after they'd arrived, Hutchins and the boys said hello to Father Huntley, who ran the dances there. Father Huntley asked Hutchins if he'd play basketball for OLA this year, and Hutchins said he didn't know. The boys wandered off to dance.

In between dancing and talking, the boys drank, in the men's room, nipping a bottle of Seagram's 7 they'd bought on the way and snuck in. Hutchins had at least three swigs of that during the night. They also drank cups of Coca-Cola served at the dance.

Around 10:15 p.m., Father Huntley asked Rogers if he'd been drinking; Rogers admitted he had. The priest walked away, like it was no big deal, and eventually found Hutchins. He talked to Hutchins for a few minutes, Rogers testified. The prosecutor wanted to make it seem like Huntley had ordered Hutchins to leave, because his breath reeked of alcohol, but Rogers said they just talked about sports. Hutchins at the time was boxing in an amateur league, and Huntley asked about his training. He asked again if Hutchins would play basketball this year, for OLA or anybody else. Then he walked away, and Hutchins joined his friends.

A few minutes later, around 10:30 p.m., Huntley told him he shouldn't drink if he were in training and again walked away. Hutchins's hands began to shiver. He hit Huntley under the shoulder with his right hand, knocking the priest on his ass. Then Hutchins threw himself to the floor, face forward, landing on his own head. He was shaking, punching the floor, slamming his head against the floor. The music stopped.

Huntley got up and tried to hold him, but he couldn't; then a Port Authority cop who happened to be there intervened, and Hutchins, now on his back, swung at him wildly, trying to push him away. The cop wrestled Hutchins and a few other men helped hold him down. Hutchins resisted, trying to use his hands and feet to get them off of him. The cop got on top of Hutchins and handcuffed his wrist, dragged him twenty-five feet to a banister and snapped the other cuff around it.

Hutchins, standing up near the banister, was near a wired plate-glass window. He put his head and hand through it. Then he hollered for the next fifteen minutes, demanding to be released. Finally he quieted down and the cop uncuffed him. People suggested calling an ambulance, but Hutchins refused, saying he felt all right.

He couldn't remember everything that'd happened. His friends walked him home, along the way informing him that he'd hit a priest. The next day he went to Father Huntley to apologize.

He said he was ashamed.

Several people, including Hutchins's fiancée, testified to witnessing Hutchins have epileptic episodes throughout the early 1950s—two while he was deployed in Japan. Among the most notable: a few months after the OLA incident, at Joe and Howard's, the ice-cream parlor where Patsy Hylan was last seen alive, Hutchins met Rogers for coffee. When they went out front after twenty minutes to fool around with some kids, Tommy "started to swing out, and he fell—he put himself on the ground," Rogers testified. "[He swung] with his hands and head, and anything he had." The owners held him down until the cops came. When Hutchins came out of it, he didn't remember what had happened. He asked his friends how he'd gotten the cuts on his hands.

Before both of these incidents, Hutchins had a similar episode. This time, police officers, as well as a few friends, had to hold him down while he used profane language and tried to kick them off. It happened one afternoon on 72nd Street, around the corner from the Bay Ridge Theater, the block on which he would later lead police to his bloody car.

"He was swinging wild," Jerome Jones said. "He was on the ground, and the cops were pinning him down, and he was, you know, trying to get on his feet again, trying to get them off him." Before police arrived, Hutchins had been smashing his head against a wall; his best friend, James Warner, stuck a lighter in Hutchins's mouth. The episode ended with police loading an exhausted Hutchins into an ambulance—which took him to Coney Island Hospital, where Patsy Hylan would die a few years later.

Warner stayed with Hutchins. At one point, a doctor told Warner, "He shouldn't drink at all."

123

Before the theater incident, Hutchins and Warner had had six or seven beers apiece at the Melody Room; before the church dance, Hutchins had also had a few. "I could tell," Warner, who'd split up from the boys for a date, testified. "I smelled it on him." There were other incidents, too, such as a basketball game in Flatbush at which Hutchins started shaking and swinging violently; Warner wasn't sure if Hutchins had been drinking before that. But before the incident in front of Joe & Howard's, Rogers had smelled the alcohol on him.

"He seemed, like, to pass out," Warner testified about these episodes, which could last from fifteen minutes to a few hours, "and he recovered, and he would not know anything that happened to him...He was in a confused state of mind...He didn't know anything—like, he would ask me what happened."

In October 1957, during Patricia Hylan's murder trial, the court staged an experiment. Hutchins was brought to Kings County Hospital for an alcohol provocative test. He was seated in a reclining chair, connected to an EEG, had his blood sugar checked and then was given three ounces of rye, mixed with three ounces of orange juice and three teaspoons of sugar. Thirty minutes later, he was given another.

Nine minutes after that, "His lips started quivering, his left hand began shaking and the EEG wires came off his head," according to a summary of the case. "His whole body then went into motion and he slid partially off the chair. He then started shaking his head very wildly and banged it against the chair. He became so violent that four correction officers could not hold him down and had to handcuff one of his arms to the chair. He fought these and other officers and shouted and screamed unintelligibly. His pupils were dilated and his reaction to light was sluggish. After this violent state subsided, defendant was bewildered and dazed. It was not possible to communicate with him for some thirty minutes, and he was confused and exhausted."

When he came to, he said he couldn't remember anything that had just happened.

After a three-week trial, the all-male jury deliberated twelve hours before convicting Hutchins of the first-degree murder of Patricia Hylan, willful and premeditated. They did not recommend mercy, which automatically sentenced him to death in the electric chair, though the formal sentencing did not take place until December, at which point the indictment for Dorothy Cameron's murder was suspended.

Hutchins spent the next sixteen months in Sing Sing before the Court of Appeals ruled, five to two, to reverse the conviction because the justices believed the prosecution had failed to prove Hutchins was sane when he killed Hylan. To be guilty of first-degree murder, the people had to prove that Hutchins had not been having an epileptic seizure when Hylan was killed. Even if Hutchins was a fiend, according to this reasoning, or "a high grade moron," as the psychologists had said, it could have been his neurological condition that made him a murderer—not his free will.

Prosecutors began preparing the case against Hutchins for the murder of Dorothy Cameron. A jury had even been selected, and then Hutchins agreed to a plea: he would cop to two counts of first-degree manslaughter, one for Patricia Hylan, the other for Dorothy Cameron. On March 16, he was sentenced to twenty-to-forty years in Sing Sing. Two days later, on March 18, he began his term.

He'd be out in fourteen.

The day before Halloween, in 1973, Thomas Hutchins walked out of Sing Sing on parole, after 5,705 days in prison—six years shy of his minimum sentence. Once condemned to death, he instead emerged free into a cool and rainy day in Ossining.

He was 39 years old.

Epilogue

In 1973, a Brooklyn-born man named Thomas Hutchins started a business in Chicago, which became a successful plumbing supplier. An undated photo of him on the company's website shows an uncanny resemblance to Patsy and Dorothy's killer, though of course he's older, and he has dark hair, not blond. His birthday, as it's listed in an obituary, is just a few days away from the killer's, as it's listed in the New York State Department of Corrections database.

This Thomas Hutchins died in Evanston Hospital in March 2006 from lung cancer, leaving behind a widow whose (albeit common) first name was the same as the middle name of the killer's fiancée at the time of the murders in 1957, as well as four sons and two daughters (and fourteen grandchildren and two great grandchildren). The eldest son was born in 1958, the year after the murders.

This Thomas Hutchins had married in 1956, according to his obituary, and started his career working for a laundry company before running a factory floor for a linen company and setting sales records for a faucet company.

In the 1980s, this Hutchins joined Alcoholics Anonymous and successfully sponsored many others, which was one of his proudest achievements. His friends in the program said he changed thousands of lives through his work there.

This Hutchins's "philosophy in life was that every day was a blessing to be cherished," according to his obituary.

"His favorite saying was, 'Have a great day in paradise!'"

Afterword

This book happened by accident. I was writing a lot about Bay Ridge history—such as how Owl's Head Park came to be—and digging deep into old newspaper archives, every once in a while stumbling onto an adjacent local crime story. I started collecting them in a file, and soon I realized I had a lot of them—and started looking for more.

Crime stories have long interested me, though I was turned off by the tawdry Mafia tell-alls that until recently seemed to define "true crime" in bookstores. When the podcast *Serial* came out, I was hooked just like so many others, and when a boom in such stories followed, I became more interested in how and why people tell them, sometimes working through my feelings in criticism for Mark Asch at *Brooklyn Magazine*.

Crime is a part of every New York community, even the safest, which people can forget. After a recent murder in Bay Ridge, the response on some social media was hysterical, along the lines of, "Can I raise my family in Bay Ridge anymore? Is it safe for us to stay?"

Of course it was—and is. The tragedy was isolated. People have been shot at, kidnapped and killed in Bay Ridge since at least the nineteenth century. Bodies used to wash up on the shore with regularity—such a story is one of the earliest mentions of "Bay Ridge" in the Brooklyn *Eagle* archives, and similar tales appeared frequently in the newspaper record into the 1980s. I hope this book is a reminder that crime occurs occasionally, and we shouldn't let it scare us as a community into moving away or hiding indoors (although we should always demand justice, especially for the families affected by it).

These stories also attracted me as a historian. In the details, they reveal so much: how people once spent their days, what they wore, where they worked, why they got up in the morning. These eleven stories show us, between the lines, what everyday life was once like in Bay Ridge, as well as the dramatic ways in which it changed over the course of almost a hundred years.

In that respect, the greatest influence on this book is a little-remembered 1984 collection I picked up randomly at the old Community Bookstore (R.I.P.) on Court Street—Calvin Trillin's *Killings*, featuring sixteen articles he wrote mostly in the '70s for *The New Yorker* while traveling around the country, reporting on local murders and, in the process, showing readers what it was like at those times to live and also die in those places—giving us a glimpse of lifestyles we'd never live in towns we'd never see. I was also inspired by *Brooklyn Noir 3*, edited by Tim McLoughlin, which introduced me to the idea that there were many forgotten, historical true-crime stories that happened where I live. (McLoughlin was kind to read an early version of this book and offer support, for which I'm grateful.)

We're attracted to true crime for the ways it lets us flirt with death, which is otherwise so mysterious and terrifying. We flirt that much more intimately when the crimes happened on streets we walk down everyday.

—Henry Stewart, December 2017

Acknowledgements

To my parents, Robin and Dave, who moved to Bay Ridge before I was born.

To Grandma, on whose living-room floor in Middle Island, Long Island, I used to flip through *The Bay Ridge Chronicles*. Her copy is now my copy.

To Michael, my friend since first grade at P.S. 185, who designed the cover.

To John, who let me tell some of these stories in his bar.

To Ben, who listened while I explained the book, once while stumbling down Narrows Avenue after a storm and again on the Old Croton Aqueduct Trail.

To Hey Ridgers past and present: Alaric, Kayla, John (again), Allison, David, Michael (again) and especially, especially Brian.

To Ted, who got me involved with the Bay Ridge Historical Society, as well as Tom, Peter and Pamela.

To the Brooklyn Public Library, which digitized the Brooklyn *Eagle* archives.

But most of all to Sam, whose talent and intelligence inspire me and whose love gives me purpose. There'd be no book—there'd be no Henry—without her.

56938818R10077

Made in the USA
Middletown, DE
25 July 2019